To Dad and Mom

For your unconditional love, guidance, and support

My dad always says, "You are who you surround yourself with." No book is ever written without the help of many. To those of you who have chosen to surround me, I am very grateful!

First, I want to thank God for the opportunity to help young women everywhere understand the importance of a real, vibrant love relationship with Jesus Christ. A relationship that is as important to me as the air I breathe.

To my parents for helping me conceptualize and organize the desire in my heart to impact young women. I love you and appreciate your example as parents who love Jesus and have helped me make smart choices in life.

To Laura Faidley—without you this book would still be a dream. Your tireless efforts brought Smart Girls, Smart Choices to life.

Likewise, a special thanks to the Harvest House team, specifically to Carolyn McCready and Terry Glaspey, for your continual commitment to me and to the young women who desire to live according to the Word of God. Gene Skinner, thank you for your time and effort in editing and for taking the manuscript to the next level!

To all of my friends. Thank you for doing life with me. We must never forget that God's love for us endures forever. Let's be Christ followers together.

And a special thanks to my brother, Zach, for your love, support, and the many, many laughs we share in life together. You continually bring me joy. Stay in love with Jesus.

Contents

Introduction

*The beauty of a girl cannot be mimicked, fabricated,
or created by human means, it only occurs naturally.*

PAM CALLAGHAN

O h, the joys and trials of being a girl! I'm so glad God created me as a woman, but sometimes life can be really hard. Every girl has issues. Insecurities. Fears.

And even when we try to hide our struggles behind a perfect facade, our hearts cry out for answers. *Who am I, and what is my life supposed to be about?*

Face it. Navigating life can be pretty tricky for us girls. We can easily get tripped up by so many things: love, intimacy, sex, emotions, peer pressure, friends, self-esteem, dreams for the future…you name it.

So what's a girl to do? Sometimes when I stop and think about the big impact of my decisions, I get a little bit scared. Do you ever feel that way?

The good news is that you and I don't have to hide our issues. We don't have to pretend to be perfect. And we don't have to go through life on our own.

The God of the universe wants to pull you and me up out of the mire of self-absorption and walk beside us as we figure out life, even when we fail, when we mess up, when we get muddy and bruised, and when we are overcome by shame and guilt.

God is there in the midst of our tears, our heartache, and our pain. He loves every single one of His daughters, and He created us to know Him, to delight in Him, to be free.

Maybe you feel weird, as if you don't fit in anywhere. But to God, no one is an outcast.

Maybe you think you've messed up so badly that God could never forgive you. But God doesn't love you because of what you do. He adores you simply because you're you. Whatever you might be facing, this book is for you as a young woman. And I want you to know that you're not alone as you struggle.

I sat down to write this little book with one goal: To get real. To push past big, abstract spiritual words and dig into the real issues that young women face today. I want to address the struggles we girls face and discover the truth from God's Word that will help us to live free in real life. God's truth is applicable to every situation and every struggle you and I face—at school, at home, at the movies, with friends, shopping, on a date…everywhere.

In each chapter, you'll read about real girls with real problems, girls I've had the privilege of meeting all across the country. Girls just like you and me. I've changed their names and altered a few insignificant details in order to protect their identities. I hope you can identify with these girls as they share about their gut-honest struggles.

I'm not into being fake. Let's get to the heart of what life is all about. Unless you and I get real about our struggles, insecurities, and fears, we'll end up making the same stupid choices over and over and over again.

God never intended for us girls to go through life solo. But we often hide because we're desperately afraid of letting anyone into the deep places of our hearts. And so we drown in loneliness and despair. We lose hope. We do foolish things and destroy our lives, our dreams, and even our futures.

God created us girls for so much more! More than just existing. More than just getting by.

I'm not an expert on life. I'm just like you—I want to follow God, I want to love Him, I want to live for Him…and yes, I'm still figuring out what that means. Still, I do know one thing: You don't have to be perfect or have a 4.0 or go to Bible school to really know Jesus.

All you need is a willing, humble heart. A heart that listens. A heart that soaks up God's Word. A heart that belongs to Jesus. A smart girl doesn't have life all figured out; she just knows the source of life—Jesus.

As you and I struggle through the challenges of being young women in today's world, we can't ignore God. He alone knows the deepest longings of our hearts and loves us perfectly. He alone sets us free from living for other people and gives us the opportunity to know Him intimately.

What are we waiting for? Let's stop running after things that don't matter, and let's stop just talking about running after God. Let's actually *run*. Let's wrestle with the real issues. Let's do what Romans 12:1 says: "Take your everyday, ordinary life—your sleeping, eating, going-to-work, and walking-around life—and place it before God as an offering."

Let's be smart.

Know too that I am praying for you. I do believe that God has a special plan—a special dream for your life. And He promises that if you seek Him, you will find Him when you search for Him with all of your heart.

Blessings,

Megan

Crazy for Love

*What if you have a genuine and captivating beauty
that is marred only by your striving?*

STASI ELDREDGE

Eight p.m. Monday night. Time to put down the homework, pop the popcorn, grab my girlfriends, and turn on today's most popular reality dating show: *The Bachelor.*

In a crazy lineup of exotic dates, 25 women take a chance at winning the handsome young bachelor's heart. We are drawn in to the delightful suspense and argue about who *we* think the bachelor will present with the rose and ask to be his soul mate. Laughing, crying, and sighing as the romance unfolds, we join these girls on their emotional roller coaster of searching for true love.

Oh, the drama, the tension, the emotions. "I came here to find love," Michelle declared to Jake. "I really, really, really want a husband." Could this be her chance at happily ever after? Apparently not. Her dreams of a future with Jake vanished along with the hopes of 24 other girls who are desperate for love.

And ah, the fickle, fun fantasy of relationships! Now in its fourteenth season, *The Bachelor* has captured the hearts of women around the world because it shows real women who are desperate to get guys' attention. I like watching this show with my friends because on some level, I can identify with these women. I long to be loved, accepted, cherished, and chosen. Don't you?

We girls love to talk about guys, flirt with them, and chase after them. But when our lives become obsessed with getting guys' attention, we're headed for trouble, just like some of these bachelorettes who get a sudden case of the stupids.

In this chapter, we'll see what desperation looks like, and we'll consider a better alternative. We'll find that we can rediscover ourselves by embracing the fact that God deeply loves and cherishes us.

Defining Desperation

So what does it mean to be desperate? Dictionary.com defines *desperate* as an attitude: "reckless or dangerous because of despair or urgency, extreme or excessive." Desperation can drive a girl to do some wild, crazy, and destructive things just to feel loved and wanted.

Of course, God created all of us to be loved and wanted. The defining characteristic of desperation, however, is that we'll often do whatever is necessary to feel that love *now*. The sense of urgency takes over because we think that if we don't get him now, we may miss out on our chance for love and end up single and alone for the rest of our lives.

So what do we do? We often mistake feelings of attraction for true love. We fall for the incredibly hot but shallow guy. We share deep secrets of our hearts prematurely. We confuse sex with love. We ditch lifelong friends for the new Prince Charming. And we ignore our parents' and mentors' advice.

When we feel desperate, we begin thinking with our emotions and not our brains. Sure, when the cutie in class or the ripped guy at the gym turns his head, we *feel* good. It's fun and exciting. The attention of a guy (especially a hottie!) holds great power over a girl's life. And nothing is wrong with that in the right context. But when we're desperate, we will do *anything* just to keep a guy in our lives.

Desperation can cause us to lose our objectivity, so we think and do things we never dreamed. And I'm not just talking about sex. Even if we technically remain virgins, giving away our bodies and the deep places of our hearts can leave lifelong scars.

These are some of the crazy things we often do when we're crazy for a guy's love and attention:

> become clingy and obsessed with him
>
> change who we are to make him happy
>
> put all our confidence in what he says
>
> become willing to do anything for him

    tolerate his rude and mean behavior

    ignore red flags

    become blind to his weaknesses

    assume that this is as good as it gets

We girls will often stay in horrible relationships because we feel trapped. Love is powerful, but it can also hurt like crazy. When *he* moves on, we are left more desperate than ever. And alone.

Getting to Know Desperate Dana

"Guess what I'm doing Friday?" Dana asked excitedly. Without waiting for an answer, she blurted out, "Hanging with Jared! Yeaahh!" She broke into a little song and dance, and with glowing eyes, she confided to me, "You know, Megan, I think he's the one. I really do. He…he told me the other day that he loves me!

"Ah…Friday night! I can't wait!" She bubbled on. "We're going out to Olive Garden and then going to a movie, and then…well, we'll just see."

"What about the sleepover at my house?" I asked her. "I thought you were coming."

"Well…I mean, I'm not going to turn Jared down. He's such a great guy…and sooooo cute! Are you kidding me? You guys enjoy your chick flick."

Desperate Dana! Listening to her dream on and on made my heart sink, and not just because she had blown us off. I'd heard Dana say the same thing about a different guy just a few weeks earlier and of yet another only three months before that. She was so desperate for the attention of a guy—any guy. Sure, we all like to be noticed, to be beautiful and wanted, but Dana's longing for a boyfriend had a lot of stupid in it. Ever had a friend like that?

A few weeks later, Dana gave me the news I had expected to hear. "Jared dumped me. Megan, I gave him everything. What do I do? I don't know who I am anymore. I can't keep living like this. I hate guys. I hate myself. What's wrong with me? Why can't I just be normal and find a boy-friend who will love me?"

In Dana's mind, her life was over. Breakups always hurt, but when we build our identities on our relationships with guys, we have no idea who we are without them. Our hopes and dreams shatter when things don't work out, and life becomes a big black hole of hopelessness.

We feel insecure, empty, depressed, wounded, and desperately alone. The ache just won't go away, and no amount of Ben and Jerry's will make it better. The only relief from the excruciating pain seems to be to throw ourselves at the next guy who comes along. We're acting like Desperate Dana.

GIRLS LIKE YOU AND ME HAD THIS TO SAY ABOUT BOYS...

"I'm learning that I can still live and breathe without a boyfriend."
—KELLY

"All the girls you're jealous of because they are prettier, skinnier, more popular, or richer than you...well, they're just as insecure as you are."
—LAUREN

"Be committed to Christ. Don't search for boys— seek Christ, and the boy you want will find you."
—TRACY

"Your value does not rest on others' opinions of you. Your value is inestimable because you are a child of the King."
—LAUREN

"God has created you to be uniquely you. Be yourself, and don't change for any guy."
—SUSAN

So what's the big deal about boys? What's so important about the way we do relationships? I was a little shocked when I saw this recent post on a chat website: "I am a cute 11-year-old girl, and I am desperate for a boyfriend." Romantic relationships may seem like innocent fun, but we girls can easily feel incomplete or less-than if we can't snag and keep a guy's attention. Looking for acceptance and security in a boyfriend often leads us to compromise and do things we said we'd never do.

- Nearly one third of girls (including preteens) see oral sex as "a fun, bonding thing to do with a guy."[1]
- One study of kids from a Midwestern high school showed that a little more than half the students were sexually active, and the average age of initiation was 15. Sexual networks were common.[2]

What's the pressure behind this trend toward sexual activity? Statistics from the Kaiser Family Foundation show that many girls confuse sex with love.

- Nearly a third of all teens feel pressured to have sex.
- A third of sexually active young women report being in a relationship where they felt things were moving too fast sexually.
- One fourth of sexually active young women report doing something sexual they didn't really want to do.

What's tragic about this picture? By the time most girls have walked across the stage to receive their high school diploma, they will have lost their virginity—and their sense of who they are. You might be thinking, *Megan, you're being old-fashioned.* No, I'm just committed to doing relationships according to the Bible. When we do, we honor God, we respect ourselves, and we build our self-esteem. We also carry a lot less baggage with us when we get married someday!

In fact, surveys of sexually active teenagers show that 55 percent of the boys and 70 percent of the girls wish they had waited longer to have sex. They are significantly more likely to be unhappy and feel depressed than teens who are not sexually active. One in four sexually active young women contracts an STD each year, and more than 1 million teenagers get pregnant each year.[3]

But the biggest wounds we carry are deep in our hearts. Whether we have been sharing the deep secrets of our hearts or making out, when the fun is over and the guy moves on, we girls are left to pick up the broken pieces. Many of us starve ourselves, binge and purge, change our hair and fashion style, and even cut ourselves because we didn't get the guy's attention.

We put ourselves through this madness in the hopes of being beautiful enough to catch Mr. Right. Maybe you can identify with one of these struggles. Let me tell you, there is a better way.

Desperate Dana and You

"I don't know who I am anymore." Dana's gut-wrenching cry reveals that her desire to be loved had led time and again to a broken heart. What about you? Does Dana's story sound familiar? Are you desperate for love? Are you insecure in who you are? Here's a little quiz that will help you find out. Take the time to write down your response to each question and think about it.

1. Am I consumed with getting guys' attention?

2. Do I have trouble talking to guys without flirting?

3. Do I hang out only with guys, or do I have solid friendships with girls too?

4. What am I communicating through my words and body language?

5. Do I want to be viewed as a sexy babe with a great body or as a beautiful and God-centered girl?

6. Do I dress in a way that accentuates my natural beauty, or does my fashion style shout, "Look at my body!" Am I all body, no brains?

7. Do I build my sense of worth and significance on the things guys say to me?

8. (If you are not in a relationship right now) Am I content being single? Do I feel incomplete without a boyfriend?

9. Do I have a timeline for getting into a relationship? Am I totally obsessed with looking for prospects?

10. (If you are dating) Do I define myself by my boyfriend? Am I possessive or controlling?

How did you do? I'm no scientific expert, but let's be honest. If a few of these questions raised red flags, you may just be a little desperate. Hey, welcome to life on this planet! The good news is that desperate Dana and the rest of us are not doomed to a life of failed relationships and unrequited love.

We can develop a more healthy way of interacting with guys. We can enjoy friendships with the young men God has placed in our lives. We can have godly and passionate dating relationships. But these things don't start with the guys.

When I was younger, I would lie in bed and ask my dad if he thought I would ever find someone to love me. He would just smile and say, "Sooner than you think—and I can't wait to meet him."

Have you ever laid in bed late at night overcome by the fear of being alone? Have you ever cried yourself to sleep over the "man of your dreams" who wouldn't even notice you? Has your heart ever soared at the sight of him, only to be crushed when you found out he already had a girlfriend?

These things are normal. We're made for love and companionship. In Genesis 2:18, God says, "It's not good for the Man to be alone." From the very beginning, woman was created for intimacy with God and man. Eve was created for Adam, and God called it good.

We create problems when we try to fulfill our need for love and acceptance solely in a guy, forgetting that God Himself is wildly in love with us. In the Bible, God says, "I've never quit loving you and never will" (Jeremiah 31:3). You and I will never have a healthy, balanced view of guy-girl relationships until we learn to be in a relationship with our heavenly Father.

God created you uniquely as a woman with the powerful desire to be known and loved for who you are. Our souls cry out for intimacy, and I don't just mean sex. As others have said, *intimacy* can be pronounced "into-me-see."

At the core of who we are, we long for someone to cherish us, rejoice over us, and love us extravagantly. We want to be known for who we are the way God knows and loves us. We naturally look for that intimacy in relationships with guys, but the truth is that no guy can fulfill the deepest longings in our hearts. Even if he says the three magical words *I love you*, he cannot really love you enough to satisfy your soul.

The most important thing to understand first is how much God loves you. Imagine Him saying to you, "I love you, daughter. You are precious and beautiful to Me. I'll do anything to include you in the church, My bride. I'll die for you." And that's exactly what He did. God sent His Son Jesus, who took God's punishment for you on a wooden cross and died an inconceivably painful death so you could live forever with Him.

Now *that's* what I call love.

One of my favorite verses is Zephaniah 3:17-18 (NIV):

> The Lord your God is with you,
>   he is mighty to save.
> He will take great delight in you,
>   he will quiet you with his love,
>   he will rejoice over you with singing.

Stop and think about this and let it sink into your heart: *God* loves you. God *loves* you. God loves *you*. Very few of us know what this really means. Understanding and believing this verse can be really hard if your dad or boyfriend tells you you're no good, if he offers you love only when you perform perfectly, or if he ignores you, abuses you, or maybe even walked out on you.

If you have been hurt by men in your life, God's love may not make sense for a while. Sometimes we're afraid to accept God's love because we associate God with the guys we know. To really "get" God's love, we have to understand He is not at all like the guys who hurt us, and His love is nothing like theirs. God's love is perfect and unconditional—and it does not depend on what we do.

At the root of it all, desperation in relationships stems from good desires gone bad. *I just want someone to love me*, our hearts cry out. That desire is from God Himself, who created our hearts. In a prayer to God, Augustine wisely wrote, "You have made us for yourself, and our heart is restless until it rests in you."[4]

Stop for a minute. Take a breath and think about what you're doing. The God of the universe delights in you. He is actually pursuing you. He has made each one of us to be perfectly satisfied and complete in Him—when we seek Him. "If you seek GOD, your God, you'll be able to find him if you're serious" (Deuteronomy 4:29). Speaking of his relationship with God, King David says, "My heart leaps for joy" (Psalm 28:7 NIV). David realized that knowing God intimately is better than anything we can imagine: "In your presence there is fullness of joy; at your right hand are pleasures forevermore" (Psalm 16:11 ESV). God promises that He will never leave you or forsake you (Joshua 1:5)! No guy can promise you that.

> You've spent your whole life running and running, trying to catch up with something that has never been there for you. And all you've done is go farther and farther away from the precious love that's been waiting for you all the time.
> **ANONYMOUS**

Your Ticket Out

We girls can be desperate for several reasons, and each reason can lead to even more problems.

- We can draw our worth and value from getting guys' (or a specific guy's) attention. When we don't get that affirmation, we feel worthless.

- We can be overwhelmed by the fear of being alone and think no guy will ever love us. So we do anything to stay in a relationship—even a bad one—just to avoid feeling lonely.

- We can try to put a Band-Aid on the wounds in our hearts by jumping into new relationships. The sparks of romance may dull our pain, but we forget that even the best guy can't fix our broken hearts. Only God can.

So what's a girl to do?

I dream for the day when my knight in shining armor will come, sweep me off my feet with his strong arms, and draw me close for a kiss. When he says "I love you," his words will communicate more than a warm, fuzzy feeling. My prince's love for me will blossom as he asks, "Megan, will you marry me?" The music will soar as I ride off into the sunset by his side into the world of happily ever after...

Okay, enough Disney. But you think about it too, don't you! We just need to balance our dreams with a solid understanding of God's love for us.

> Perfect intimacy,
> unconditional acceptance,
> faultless righteousness,
> and direct access to your King's presence 24/7.
> He will never stop loving you,
> always fight for you,
> and never let you down—
> no matter what.

By now you may be thinking, *I understand the whole God thing, Megan. I love God. But I just need a guy. I can't imagine my life without a boyfriend. I want to feel his touch and know his love is real.*

Let me challenge you one more time: What does an un-desperate girl look like? If you look in the dictionary, you will find that the opposite of being desperate is being confident, content, satisfied, secure, unworried… and the list goes on. The un-desperate girl is free to become the woman God wants her to be because she isn't consumed with getting guys' attention.

So how do we do it? How do we break free from desperation and learn to live as God's girls?

Anchor Your Life in God

Do you believe that the One who created these desires for love and romance in our hearts, who knows every hair on our heads, who gave us eyesight to read these words…is He able to bring the right guy into our lives too? Don't you think He—the Creator of romance—can write a love story that's *way* better than anything we could come up with?

Being God's girl starts with pursuing the one true love of our lives—Jesus—rather than chasing after guys. Living our life for a guy may make us happy for a time, but it won't satisfy our souls. Only Jesus can do that.

Despite our good intentions, we *will* go back to reckless chaos unless we choose to follow Jesus Christ with all that we have. We get to know Him by spending time with Him, so read the Bible, meditate on it, and hide its truth in your heart. Find a good devotional. Find some girls who get it too.

I know this isn't easy to do, but the Bible says, "Steep your life in

God-reality, God-initiative, God-provisions. Don't worry about missing out. You'll find all your everyday human concerns will be met" (Matthew 6:33)…including your concerns about guys.

Remember, we always make time for what's important to us. So don't just *talk* about chasing after God. Run for Him! And as you do, realize that following God may mean leaving some things (and some people) behind. Remember, you live to please God, not a guy.

Reject the "You Complete Me" Lie

The "you complete me" myth sells movies, music, books, and magazines, but it can give us really messed-up ideas about who we are. This is what the Bible says: "Don't be wishing you were someplace else or with someone else. Where you are right now is God's place for you. Live and obey and love and believe right there. God, not your marital status, defines your life" (1 Corinthians 7:17).

God knows what He's doing. He knows the deepest desires of our hearts. And because He created us, He also knows that no guy can ever complete us. Here's the way my dad describes it:

incomplete woman + incomplete man = incomplete,
dysfunctional relationship

but

complete woman + complete man = complete,
God-honoring relationship

God has a dream for our lives, but it's not just about getting what *we* want. It's about us glorifying God with every single part of who we are—even in our relationships with guys.

Sometimes we girls are confused and don't understand what God is doing. Honestly, sometimes I wonder why it takes so crazy long for God to bring the right guy along. But when we feel that way, we can rest assured that where we are is God's place for us right now.

Talk to God About Everything

Living as God's girls includes talking honestly with God about the deepest needs of our hearts. Rather than always running to guys for affirmation when we are stressed, upset, worried, or depressed, we can pour out our hearts to God, knowing that He hears our words and sees our tears, and He treasures them.

Think about it—God wants us to talk with Him as we would with a wonderful dad. He is ready and waiting to listen to us. Why would we *not* talk to Him?

David is one of my favorite Bible characters because He didn't hold back. He talked to God about everything. And I mean *everything.* Angry, happy, despairing, or ecstatic, David was blabbing on to God. How could he be so bold? Well, look what he knew.

> You've kept track of my every toss and turn
>> through the sleepless nights,
> Each tear entered in your ledger,
>> each ache written in your book (Psalm 56:8).

Every ache, every tear, every sleepless night…regardless of the craziness we feel, we can talk to God about it. Whether you're sad, mad, angry, upset, or hurting, don't hesitate any longer. Run to Him! Don't worry, God isn't scared off by our drama or our brokenness. He already knows our hearts, and He desperately wants to satisfy us with His unfailing love. God specializes in healing broken hearts and fixing messed-up lives in a way no guy ever could.

Treasure and Guard Your Intimacy

Attraction is a powerful force. As women, our bodies are powerful tools created uniquely by God to be stunningly beautiful and irresistible to our husbands. God made us to be beautiful. But until we say "I do," we show respect for ourselves and the guys around us by valuing our bodies.

Now, don't get me wrong. I love my heels, my pearls, and a little lipstick. Looking good and feeling confident in our beauty is great. I love dressing up, mixing and matching the latest fashions to get my own unique look. We don't need to be ashamed of our bodies. God never tells us to wear shapeless sacks, but Scripture does tell us to honor God with our bodies (1 Corinthians 6:20).

But the way I attract a guy determines what he will love me for. I don't know about you, but I want to be loved for more than just my looks, my cute outfits, and my heels. I want a husband who will also treasure my heart.

Guarding our intimacy is not just about what we wear. It also involves what we say and don't say. Keeping our emotions in check is an important part of treasuring our intimacy. As God's daughter, I want to respect myself and save the deepest places of my heart for my husband rather than share those secrets with every guy who comes along.

Focus on Things That Really Matter

How many girlfriends have you lost to their boyfriends? When she met him, everything between you as friends changed. She didn't seem to care about you anymore. That's definitely not cool, and the same goes for you. Take a moment to think about everything and everyone in your life. Now read these verses:

- "A friend loves at all times" (Proverbs 17:17 NIV).
- "Carry each other's burdens" (Galatians 6:2 NIV).
- "Be devoted to one another in brotherly love" (Romans 12:10 NIV).

Regardless of how mundane our lives may seem, we can choose to look for ways to help and bless the people God has placed in our lives. Here are a few ideas:

Write an encouraging note to someone who is down.

Text your friends and ask how you can pray for them (and then pray for them!).

Bake cookies and deliver them to your neighbors.

Help out with the kids' ministry at your church.

Volunteer at a homeless shelter or soup kitchen.

Tutor underprivileged kids in your area.

Become a companion to a nursing home resident.

Organize an after-school Bible study at your school.

These are just a few options. Don't be afraid to dream big! God can use you to encourage other girls and share the gospel. You can probably think of countless ways to get outside of yourself and invest in the lives of hurting people around you. And believe me, *that* is attractive to a godly guy.

In the Word

> Lord, my longings are sitting in plain sight,
>   my groans an old story to you.
> My heart's about to break (Psalm 38:9).

Oh, the feelings we battle as young women! Romance may be one of the greatest gifts God created, but it can tear apart our hearts and hurt like crazy. The messages of our culture add to our confusion. As we struggle to find out who we are, the only secure place to start is in God's Word. Let's dive into the Bible together and find out what God has to say. These powerful truths can demolish the lies you may have believed about yourself. (They are paraphrases of the NIV.)

> You are precious and honored in God's sight (Isaiah 43:4).
>
> You are God's workmanship (Ephesians 2:10).
>
> You are more than a conqueror (Romans 8:37).
>
> You are completely forgiven (Ephesians 1:7).
>
> You are free from the law of sin and death (Romans 8:2).
>
> You are the righteousness of God in Christ Jesus
> (2 Corinthians 5:21).

It's easy to base our identity on the guy we're with, but when we truly grasp that *this* is who we are in Jesus Christ, we can be confident as God's girls rather than feel the compulsive need to get guys' attention.

Emotions like fear influence us girls a lot. Fear can steal our objectivity. It can cripple us and make obedience to God difficult. Fear can keep us in unhealthy relationships just so we won't be alone. The only force in the whole universe stronger than our fear is God's love, which is perfect. And "perfect love casts out fear" (1 John 4:18 ESV).

Are you a little bit anxious? Maybe you're downright afraid to give God control of your love life (or nonexistent love life).

Are you terrified of being alone? Of never meeting the love of your life? You're not the only one. All of us girls think about this.

But here's where we get to trust God and believe His promises. In the Bible, David told God, "When I am afraid, I will trust in You" (Psalm 56:3 NIV). Sounds simple, huh? But oh, so hard! Trusting God means resting in Him rather than trying to figure everything out on our own.

Regardless of how alone we feel, we are never ever alone. "I'll never let you down, never walk off and leave you," God tells us (Hebrews 13:5). When we feel overwhelmed and paralyzed by fear, we can take it to Jesus. He already knows our hearts, and He promises to never leave us or forsake us.

God can handle our fears. In the Bible, David writes, "Even there your hand will guide me, your right hand will hold me fast" (Psalm 139:10 NIV). Where is *there*? It's wherever you are right now. Even in a place of confusion, desperation, loneliness, or whatever, God is holding your hand. Imagine Him saying this to us, His girls:

> I know what I'm doing. I have it all planned out—plans to take care of you, not abandon you, plans to give you the future you hope for.
>
> When you call on me, when you come and pray to me, I'll listen.
>
> When you come looking for me, you'll find me.
>
> Yes, when you get serious about finding me and want it more than anything else, I'll make sure you won't be disappointed (Jeremiah 29:11-14).

No joke, being alone is tough sometimes. But pursuing Jesus first and basking in His love for us will save us from a lot of bad decisions and subsequent heartache. With God and a few good girlfriends, we can make it.

We looked at Psalm 38:9 earlier. This is what David goes on to say:

> What I do, GOD, is wait for you,
>   wait for my Lord, my God—you will answer!
> I wait and pray (verse 15).

Smart Girls Remember...

We'll conclude each chapter by summarizing a few of the most important points and providing a prayer you can use.

- Having a boyfriend will not complete you as a woman. Only by knowing who you are in Jesus Christ will you ever be whole, complete, and confident.

- If you live your life to make other people happy, you will never be wholly satisfied.

- Desperation will get the attention of guys who want to mess around, but it is not attractive to the kind of guy you want to marry.

- Guys tend to view desperate girls as easy, trashy, and cheap.

- Who you are is not wrapped up in what you look like or what you do. Who you are is defined by *whose* you are, and you belong to God.

Lord Jesus,

Thank You for creating me as a woman with the desire to be known and loved. God, I mess up sometimes, and often I try to find that intimacy in a guy, forgetting that You're my first love. Remind me, Jesus, of how much You love me. Help me to learn to run to You and not to be desperate for others' attention. Set me free from this crazy desire to be noticed and affirmed by guys all the time. I want to change, God, but I need Your help. Show me how Your unconditional love is far more satisfying than a guy's infatuation. Teach me to trust You with my future.

Amen.

2

Controlled by Emotions

Just follow your heart. That's what I do.

NAPOLEON IN *NAPOLEON DYNAMITE*

Follow your heart. Three powerful words. Search Google and you'll find millions of hits for this phrase. It sounds so good, so innocent, so freeing. But it's so misleading.

I love chick-flick movie night with my girlfriends. But pick up just about any movie these days, and you're bound to hear this same message. Somewhere between the drop-dead handsome guy and the long-awaited kiss, Hollywood whispers something like this: "Do what feels good. Obey what your heart tells you. Look for answers within yourself. Stop worrying about it, and let your emotions take the wheel. After all, how could something that feels so good be wrong?"

But what happens if someone follows that advice? She turns into Ms. Drama Queen USA! In this chapter we'll find out how that happens. We'll look at the pitfalls of letting our emotions control our lives, and we'll discover how we can find our way off the emotional roller coaster and onto solid ground—a deeper knowledge of who we are as God's treasured daughters.

Defining Emotions

Emotions. We talk about them all the time, but what do we really mean? The word *emotion* literally means "to move." Taking a definition from the Web, an *emotion* is "a conscious mental reaction experienced as strong feeling usually directed toward a specific object" (or a guy!).

There are so many emotions. Just look at this tiny list I compiled:

angry	envious	nervous
anxious	excited	optimistic
ashamed	exhilarated	panicked
astonished	fearful	relieved
content	grouchy	sad
delighted	happy	scared
disappointed	humiliated	thrilled
disgusted	insecure	worried

Having emotions is part of being human and especially part of being a girl. But what does it mean to be *controlled* by our emotions? After all, there's a big difference between having a bad day and being an emotional wreck.

Honestly, sometimes my world seems out of control and I can't seem to get off the roller coaster of feelings. You've probably had those days too, when you throw yourself on your bed and cry as if the world were about to end. Sometimes emotions can seem like pure torture!

Though emotions are good and God-given gifts, if our current state of mind becomes the foundation for our decision making, we can mess up big-time. Sometimes following our gut is a good thing. But my gut feelings can change in a minute based on the number of tests I have to study for, the cafeteria food I ate earlier, the weather outside, and the song that's playing on my iPod.

We certainly shouldn't try to shut off our emotions or pretend feelings aren't there. So what do we do? We assume that our feelings are a reliable source of wisdom for life. We make decisions in the moment without stopping to think about the consequences. We view feelings as the end-all, be-all test for God's will. Feeling happy and getting what we want becomes our number one goal in life.

But we need to understand that our feelings are only *part* of who we are and not *who* we are. And trying to go through life with only our feelings to guide us can many times lead us to make stupid decisions we will later regret. Whether we're considering our future, a guy, or how we will spend our weekend, our current emotional state is not the most reliable guide to navigating the deep places of our hearts and sorting out what our true desires are.

When we don't keep our emotions in a healthy balance with our brains, we often…

> listen to ourselves more than we do to God
>
> focus on what we want and not on what we know
>
> become helpless victims of our emotions
>
> let our emotional state dictate what we do
>
> use the excuse "I don't feel like it"
>
> fail to take responsibility for our behavior
>
> fall apart when we don't get our way
>
> assume that God has left us when we don't feel Him

> Don't blindly trust your heart. It's too fragile.
> And besides, it's not on the right side.
> **ANONYMOUS**

Getting to Know Emotional Erika

"Saturday! Shopping in DC! Woot woot!" Erika high-fived me as we walked out of our last biology class of the week, and I was as excited as she was. After two tests and a lab practical, I needed a break, and I was excited to take a road trip and catch the latest spring sales with my new friend from class. Little did I know what the next few hours would hold.

Eight a.m.: "You know, life is just awesome," Erika bubbled as we cruised down the interstate singing along with Taylor Swift's "Love Story."

"We survived another week of college, hittin' the road for a day on the town…this is what I call livin'," I replied.

Twelve thirty p.m.: Hitting up Hollister, American Eagle, and Forever 21, Erika and I laughed hilariously as we tossed clothes over the dividing wall of the fitting room to each other. "Oh my gosh—you have *got* to see this top on me." Erika yelled over. "It's sweeeeeet."

As Erika modeled the pink flowered T-shirt, she blurted out, "I *love* shopping with you. I'm so glad we came today. This is so much fun."

One fifteen p.m.: Waiting in line to check out, I listened to Erika jabber on about the hottest spring styles and the latest guys in her life. I could barely get a word in edgewise, and over the grumblings of my stomach, all I could think of was *food*. Subway, Chick-Fil-A, and McDonalds signs seemed to be shouting my name.

"Okay, now on to Victoria's Secret, Bath and Body Works, Abercrombie, and Aeropostale…whew! We are rockin'!" Erika quipped.

When I hinted about lunch, Erika reacted, "Are you kidding me? We're gonna shop until we drop." On we went.

Four fifteen p.m.: Right in the middle of checking out at Hollister, Erika got a phone call—from her boyfriend. "Hi honey! How are you?" she answered. "Oh…well, I'm in DC with Megan right now shopping! We're having such a fun day!" Then the conversation turned ugly. "What! You're hanging out with who tonight?" [pause] "Unbelievable! You know I hate it when you hang with them. I can't believe you'd do that to me. Ugh." Erika slammed her phone shut without saying goodbye. "I can't believe him," she muttered. But by the time she paid for her clothes at Hollister and we were out the door, she was as chipper as could be again.

Six forty-five p.m.: Shopping had taken its toll, and I was pooped. Relaxing as we ate dinner, Erika was still talking, but the tone had turned sour as she griped about the rude attendant at Abercrombie and the poor service at Bath and Body Works.

"What the heck? You've got to be kidding me!" Erika moaned as she read a text on her phone. "My mom is ridiculous. She's trying to tell me I can't go to the movie tomorrow because we're having family dinner. Well, Mom, *that's* not gonna happen."

Eight thirty p.m.: On our way out of town, we stopped for gas and picked up drinks inside a convenience store. Coming back to the car, I was surprised to find my friend sobbing with her head on the steering wheel. "Erika, what happened?" I asked.

Through her tears, Erika blubbered, "Uhhh. I hate my life. Why did we even come on this stupid trip?" Trying to get the lid off her drink, Erika had spilled Coke down her brand-new shirt. Hitting the steering wheel in frustration, she'd broken a nail.

Not the best ending to our relaxing shopping trip to DC, huh? Look into the life of Ms. Drama Queen USA for very long, and you'll see that everything and everybody around her is spinning out of control.

GIRLS LIKE YOU AND ME HAD THIS TO SAY ABOUT EMOTIONS...

"It's easy for me to be influenced way too much by how I feel. I'm learning that this can get us girls into big trouble sometimes."
—LAUREN

"Every girl's emotions can be topsy-turvy. Whether it's PMS, a lame date, or a fight with a friend, we all have our bad days. I just don't want to be controlled by how I feel at the moment. That's craziness."
—JOSIE

"It's okay to cry! I wish someone had told me before that I didn't always have to put on a show. Don't act like you have everything together. If you need help, find it."
—TRACY

"I used to feel like I had to be all put together to talk to God. But the amazing thing is that no matter what crazy emotions we're feeling, we can cry out to God. He knows our hearts, and He'll always be there for us."
—AMY

"I'm so glad God gave us brains to balance out our emotional hearts! No matter what we're feeling—even when things seem out of control—we can be certain that God's holding us in His big, strong, loving hands."
—ANNE

When things don't work out the way you want, what do you do?

Like Erika, we can easily allow our God-given emotions to take over, which sets us up to hurt those closest to us the most. We think the world should stop and give a little consideration to the way we feel. Ever been there, in a storm of emotions where you feel entitled to be frustrated and angry? When we allow those emotions to guide our decisions, things can get crazy fast.

What's the big deal about how we feel? Why are emotions so powerful in young women's lives? Millions of people ride roller coasters each year, but many of us girls ride the roller coaster of emotions every single day.

We *feel* a craving for a big bowl of Ben and Jerry's Chocolate Mudslide at 11 p.m., so we head for the freezer. We *feel* like we're fat and ugly, so we get up early to work out, starve the next day, or start binging and purging, starving our bodies so we can *feel* beautiful.

We *feel* like our lives are out of control, so we turn to drugs and sex to drown out the pain. We *feel* worthless, so we cut ourselves and even entertain the idea of suicide.

We *feel* like sleeping in on Sunday morning rather than getting up for church, so we hit the snooze button one more time. We *feel* like God has abandoned us, so we decide to stop following Him.

Be honest. We've all experienced deep and heart-rending emotions. Maybe you can relate to some of these unhealthy ways of coping with emotional stress. Whether you gorge yourself on food, become clingy and possessive of your friends, or dull your mind with TV, your out-of-control emotions can ultimately destroy your life.

Reading about the destructive ways we young women handle our emotions, I have to question whether good feelings are actually good indicators of what is good for you and me. Can we always trust our hearts to tell us the truth? Regardless of what Hollywood says, are our feelings really the most trustworthy measure of reality?

Emotional Erika and You

From "Life is awesome" to "I hate my life." In just a few short hours, Erika's world fell apart. Her uncontrollable sobs were more than just disappointment about breaking a nail. This young woman's entire existence was controlled by the way she felt. A hangnail, a bad hair day, her boyfriend's actions, a spilled drink...just about anything had the potential to ruin Erika's day. She seemed like a helpless victim—a sailboat tossed on the waves of her emotions.

What about you? Does Erika's story sound a bit familiar? Are you controlled by your feelings? Is Ms. Emotion driving the car of your life? Here's another little quiz that will help you find out. Take the time to write down your response to each question and think about it.

1. Does the way I feel dictate what I do?

2. Do I unload my feelings on others without listening to theirs?

3. Do my friends associate me with the latest drama?

4. Do I tend to take things personally? Do I get hurt easily?

5. Do I tend to make impulsive decisions in the heat of the moment?

6. When I don't get my way or my plans fall through, is my day ruined?

7. When criticized or rejected, do I lash out and get revenge?

8. Do my friends and family tell me I am too emotional?

9. When making decisions, do I tend to rely on how I'm feeling?

10. Am I riding an emotional roller coaster? Do I live for excitement?

How did you do? If you answered yes to many of these questions, you may be living mostly out of your emotions. But here's the good news: You can get off the roller coaster. You can develop more healthy ways of dealing with your emotions. You can have a healthy relationship with your emotions without being a slave to your own heart.

> I don't want to be at the mercy of my emotions. I want to use them, enjoy them, and dominate them.
> **OSCAR WILDE**

You might be thinking, *Sounds great, Megan, but I think I'm okay. I'll be fine.*

Be honest with yourself for a minute. All of us struggle with emotions. Even the prettiest, smartest, most talented girls you know still sometimes struggle with how they feel.

When life gets stressful and our world spins out of control, we girls can be shocked and surprised at what should be a no-brainer: "Keep vigilant watch over your heart; that's where life starts" (Proverbs 4:23).

Our emotions are powerful—really powerful. Without even realizing what we're doing, we can respond to our emotional distress by turning to things that will ultimately hurt us. That's why the Bible specifically warns us to watch over our hearts, to take care of them and protect them.

So what does that look like?

Which should you trust more—your heart or your head? Good question. We need to find a balance. When I think about balance, I think of a circus tightrope walker. I don't understand how anyone could actually walk across a wire, but I do know one thing: It can't be done without a balancing tool. Every tightrope artist uses a pole of some kind to keep his center of gravity.

When we walk the tightrope of emotions, balance is impossible without the balancing pole of the Word of God. "By your words I can see where I'm going; they throw a beam of light on my dark path...Everything's falling apart on me, GOD; put me together again with your Word" (Psalm 119:105,107).

A dark path. A tightrope. A roller coaster. All of these images convey uncertainty, fear, and the need for trust. Not trust in ourselves, not confidence in our own hearts, but faith in God Himself—the One who put our hearts together when He created us.

How can we use emotions to balance our decision making? Try thinking of your emotions as signals. For instance, ask yourself questions like these:

> Why am I feeling this way?
>
> What is the belief behind this?
>
> Are my feelings based in reality?
>
> Are my thoughts a little out of control?

What can I do to appropriately calm down?

Emotions, like every other part of us, must be handed over to the control of God. Then they can be incredibly valuable.

> To ignore, repress, or dismiss our feelings is to fail to listen to the stirrings of the Spirit within our emotional life. Jesus listened. In John's Gospel we see that Jesus was moved with the deepest emotions (11:33)…The Son of Man did not scorn or reject feelings as fickle and unreliable. They were sensitive antennae to which He listened carefully and through which He perceived the will of His Father for congruent speech and action.[1]

Rather than riding the roller coaster of emotion (or trying to kill our feelings), God's girl continually chooses to put her heart's desires in God's hands because she realizes that life is *not* all about feeling good. Rather than blindly trusting our feelings, we can filter our emotions through what we *know* is true about God. "We use our powerful God-tools for smashing warped philosophies, tearing down barriers erected against the truth of God, fitting every loose thought and emotion and impulse into the structure of life shaped by Christ" (2 Corinthians 10:5).

God wants us to submit our hearts to Him because He knows that left to ourselves, we'll end up using destructive things to try to cope with the craziness of our emotions.

Your Ticket Out

We girls can be driven by our feelings for several faulty reasons.

- We can think that if we just follow our hearts, everything will turn out okay. But if we believe that, we'll base our decisions on the way we feel at the moment.

- We can be focused on self and think that being emotional is just who we are. That makes us feel entitled to vent to the world about anything and anybody.

- We can use our emotions to get attention from other people (especially guys). But if we do, we'll manipulate others with our tears and our drama to get what we want.

What's a girl to do? Maybe as you've been reading, you've been able to identify with Emotional Erika. In some way, we all can. Learning to handle our emotions in a healthy way is one of the toughest issues we women face.

Ignoring our deep feelings is not only nearly impossible but also harmful. Deep joys and crushing heartaches will come. But in order to navigate the ups and downs of life, we need a reliable guide. And I for one know that my heart is not all that dependable. We need to listen to our hearts, but making decisions solely based on the way we feel is simply not smart.

The overly emotional girl can be fun to be around for a little while. After all, she's peppy, excited, and full of life. But when hard times hit—a roommate conflict, a relationship breakup, or just a tough assignment in school—Emotional Erika's world falls apart. She doesn't know how to handle stress, so she lives at the mercy of her feelings.

In contrast, the girl whose life is grounded in her relationship with Jesus and not just in the way she feels has something to cling to even when life gets stressful. She pays attention to her heart but listens more closely to the God of her heart. She knows that regardless of the way she's feeling, God is real. God is with her. And God wants to guide her through the maze of emotions in every situation to find rest in His arms.

A young woman who is *not* a slave to her emotions is free to become the woman God wants her to be. She can ride out the waves of her heart's feelings because Jesus is at the helm. God's girl knows that the same One who said, "Peace, be still!" to the wind and the waves can also calm her anxious, fluttering heart. She is like the person the psalmist decribes in Psalm 112:7: "He will have no fear of bad news; his heart is steadfast, trusting in the LORD" (Psalm 112:7 NIV).

So how can we get off the emotional roller coaster and learn to live as God's girls?

Ground Your Heart in God's Heart

Living as God's girl includes getting in tune with God's heart. Everywhere we turn, whether to *Gilmore Girls*, Taylor Swift, or the latest Lucky Charms commercial, you and I hear the lies of self-reliance playing like a broken record: *Let your heart lead you. If it feels good, do it. Trust yourself.*

But blindly following our hearts can really mess up our lives. Rather than trusting our emotions as utterly reliable guides, we can exercise our

God-given privilege of living in tune with His heart. The Bible challenges you and me to listen to God more than we listen to our own feelings.

> Trust GOD from the bottom of your heart;
>> don't try to figure out everything on your own.
> Listen for God's voice in everything you do, everywhere you go;
>> he's the one who will keep you on track (Proverbs 3:5-6).

Getting in tune with God's heart means taking a step back from the craziness around us. We can turn off the iPod, put down the cell phone, turn off the TV, and pick up the Bible, where God has displayed His heart. We girls will never develop a deep and intimate relationship with Jesus unless we fight for it. We need to turn down the volume of everything else in our hearts and tune in to God.

Remember That You Can Control Your Emotions

If you haven't figured it out by now, we do *not* have to be victims of our emotions. "It is absolutely clear that God has called you to a free life. Just make sure that you don't use this freedom as an excuse to do whatever you want to do and destroy your freedom. Rather, use your freedom to serve one another in love" (Galatians 5:13).

We all have a selfish streak in us. Sometimes our emotions get the better of us simply because we're just focusing on ourselves and on getting what *we* want—now. But living as God's girl means living your life for more than just you. It means learning to love and care about other people, not just yourself.

But Megan, you might think, *sometimes my life is insane! What am I supposed to do then? As hard as I try, I can't control my emotions.*

And you're right. Broken nails, bad hair days, a hard test—as girls, we simply need to let go of emotions stemming from little irritations. But what about the biggies? What about heartbreak, betrayal, and loneliness? How are we supposed to handle feelings like these?

Truth is, we can't. Not in our own strength.

I want to learn to balance my emotions, but when things get crazy and out of control, I know of only one thing to do: Run to Jesus. Don't walk, don't dawdle...*run*. Jesus asks, "Are you tired? Worn out? Burned out on religion? Come to me" (Matthew 11:28). We can be sure that the God who created us and knows us intimately can definitely handle our heart's craziest feelings even when we can't.

Obey God, Not Your Feelings

Nancy Leigh DeMoss wrote, "If we accept the lie that we can't control our emotions, we will also believe we can't control how we act when we are feeling emotionally vulnerable or out of control. Not only are we too quick to believe our feelings, we are also far too quick to obey them."[2]

You and I should be aware of our emotions, but God wants His daughters to be driven by one thing alone: a desire to bring Him glory. "The love of Christ controls us," the apostle Paul wrote to followers of Jesus (2 Corinthians 5:14 ESV).

When you and I choose to obey God regardless of the way we're feeling at the moment, His heart leaps with delight. We can talk all we want about trusting Jesus, but the true test is obedience. In some really tough situations, the last thing in the world I wanted to do was obey God. Obeying God is hard sometimes. Really hard. But deeper than the tears and the pain in my heart, I knew I had to.

The reward for obedience to our heavenly Father far outweighs the struggle. Jesus tells us, "The person who knows my commandments and keeps them, that's who loves me. And the person who loves me will be loved by my Father, and I will love him and make myself plain to him" (John 14:21).

Do you want to *know* God? God wants to show us His heart. He wants to give us the joy of being in His presence. But it all starts with obeying. God's girl chooses to say, like David, "I run in the path of your commands, for you have set my heart free" (Psalm 119:32 NIV).

Even when our hearts scream no and all we want is our own way, we can be confident that obeying God will always bring glory to our Father and will eventually bring joy to our hearts.

Build Your Life on Truth

As we've seen in this chapter, emotions can be fickle. Truth, on the other hand, is solid, firm, and unchanging. Jesus tells the story of a big storm that hit two houses. The foundation of the first house was laid on solid rock. "Rain poured down, the river flooded, a tornado hit—but nothing moved that house. It was fixed to the rock." The second house was built on a sandy beach. "When a storm rolled in and the waves came up, it collapsed like a house of cards" (Matthew 7:25,27).

So how about it? Which house would you want to live in? Which one do you want your heart to be like? You're not likely to wake up tomorrow to see a tornado thundering toward your house, but you may get hit by an unexpected emotional storm. And let me tell you, you *will* occasionally get hit by crazy emotions. It's a fact. You're only human.

What can you do about it? Start building today. Right now. Will you build with bricks (God's truth) or straw (your own emotional impulses)? Here are a few bricks to get you started:

> God will never leave you or forsake you (Hebrews 13:5).
>
> You belong to God. No one can ever snatch you away (John 10:29).
>
> God started a work in your heart, and He will finish it (Philippians 1:6).
>
> Even in your darkest, scariest moments, God is there (Psalm 23:4).

In the Word

Tears, laughter, loneliness, frustration, disappointment, anger...all of these emotions are part of being human. Just look at these psalms, and you'll see David pouring his guts out to God.

> I'm at the end of my rope, my life in ruins.
>   I'm fading away to nothing, passing away...
> Help me, oh help me, GOD, my God,
>   save me through your wonderful love (Psalm 109:22-23,26).

> God, God...my God!
>   Why did you dump me
>   miles from nowhere?
> Doubled up with pain, I call to God
>   all the day long...
> My heart is a blob
>   of melted wax in my gut (Psalm 22:1-2,14).

Talk about honesty! David's heart-wrenching cries to God are refreshingly real. David didn't hide his emotions, his depression, or his anger from God. He took it all right to God and laid it out. He felt the freedom to let God in on the deep aches and yearnings of his heart. And the best part of it all is that God listened.

> My mouth's full of great praise for GOD,
>   I'm singing his hallelujahs surrounded by crowds,
> For he's always at hand to take the side of the needy
>   (Psalm 109:30-31).

I've got news for you. It really is okay to cry. Being God's girls doesn't mean we have to be strong and put-together all the time. The amazing thing about knowing God is having the freedom to be real, to spill our stuff to God about anything and everything that's going on in our hearts—guy stuff, friend stuff, family stuff, school stuff, future stuff…anything.

When we freak out about life, God doesn't. Nothing freaks Him out because He already knows about everything. Nothing surprises our God, not even the fear, anger, doubt, or anxiety of your heart.

Jesus intimately understands our weakness and our pain because He too experienced life in a broken world. His family misunderstood Him, the religious leaders rejected Him, the crowds gossiped about Him, and His close friend betrayed Him. The Romans mocked Him, beat Him, and hung Him on a cross to die. God the Father even seemed to have forsaken Him.

> We do not have a high priest who is unable to sympathize with our weaknesses, but we have one who has been tempted in every way, just as we are—yet was without sin. Let us then approach the throne of grace with confidence, so that we may receive mercy and find grace to help us in our time of need (Hebrews 14:15-16 NIV).

So talk to God. Pour your heart out to Him. Be completely honest with Him. God is never too busy for you, and He will never look down on you for being weak. He's ready and waiting to listen to you. We may try to hide the circles under our eyes and the pain in our hearts, but we can never hide from God. He sees right past the makeup, the eyeliner, and the put-together image we try to portray. And He loves us simply because we're His girls.

So what are you waiting for? Take your crazy emotions to the One who looks at lightning, wind, and rain and says, "Be still." You think He can't handle your heart? Think again.

Smart Girls Remember...

- God created emotions to complement your life, not to control you.

- Blindly following our hearts will always lead us astray because our hearts can be fickle and deceitful.

- When you're making decisions, trust the Word of God and obey what you know. Don't rely only on what you feel.

- Give your heart and your crazy emotions over to the control of God. He wants you to be fully alive and free, not tossed to and fro by every emotion you feel.

- When you freak out about life, God doesn't. You can totally trust Him to be there for you even in the storms of emotion.

Dear Lord,

My life is out of control. I need You. Thank You for creating me not only with the ability to think but also with the capacity to feel. But my emotions can be crazy sometimes, God. I so easily forget what I know is true about You and get swept away in the fear, anxiousness, or longings of the moment. It's not a matter of just trying harder, God. I can't figure out all this heart stuff on my own. I desperately need You to give me wisdom and to help me sort through my feelings and Your desires for me. I'm kind of stuck on this roller coaster of emotions. Set me free from bondage to my feelings, and show me how to submit my heart and my emotions to Your control.

Amen.

3

Consumed with Self

Once I began to notice a ton of pride, selfishness, and insecurity in my heart, the Gospel became sweeter to me.

BETHANY DILLON

There's no movie like *Mean Girls* to open your eyes to the evil reality of selfishness in our girlish hearts.

Cady Heron is 15 years old, homeschooled all her life, clueless about the social world, and the perfect target for the Plastics—the most popular, most beautiful, and cruelest girls in school.

> REGINA GEORGE: "She thinks she's gonna have a party and not invite me? Who does she think she is?"
>
> KAREN SMITH: "Oh my gosh, she's so annoying."
>
> GRETCHEN WIENERS: "I'm sorry that people are so jealous of me, but I can't help it that I'm so popular."

Though an unlikely recruit for the Plastics, Cady proves that no girl is immune from being stuck on herself. In just a few weeks, Cady is nearly a Plastic herself. Enticed by the limelight of popularity, Cady soon becomes obsessed with being the perfect girl. For the Plastics, life is all about getting attention, being number one, and using anything (like beauty and popularity) to manipulate, control, and cut down other people.

Regina, Karen, and Gretchen are not all that different from the typical American girl—full of drama and focused on self. *My life, my dreams, my plans, my friends, my future, me, me, me…*Have you ever met her? Have you ever *been* her? The truth is that we all love a little attention—okay, maybe a lot. We like to get our way and be in control. Sometimes, thinking that life is all about us is all too easy.

In this chapter, we're going to deal with a difficult but important topic—how to recognize selfishness in our hearts. We're also going to rediscover the beauty of being kind and serving others—living the kind of life Jesus lived and so often spoke of. A healthy view of ourselves is really important, but we can easily focus just on what *we* want, forgetting to see and care about others around us.

Defining Selfishness

So what is selfishness? One website defines this self-absorbed attitude as "concentrating on one's own advantage, pleasure, or well-being without regard for others." Our naturally selfish hearts can lead us to be rude, obnoxious, and downright mean just to feel better about ourselves.

But of course, we all want to feel good about ourselves. We all want to be liked, to be noticed and appreciated. The defining characteristic of selfishness, though, is that we'll do whatever we have to just to get what we want, even if that includes belittling, criticizing, or slandering other people. Ouch! Have you ever been the target of any of that? Have you ever done it yourself?

So what do we do? When we're acting out of selfishness, all we can think about is *me, me, me*. We think the world revolves around us. We obsess over being noticed and popular. We don't notice other people's needs. We put on an attitude—"be your own person"—even if that means stepping on the people closest to us. We become narrow-minded and manipulative. Rather than looking for ways to help and serve our family and friends, we may even *use* them to get our way.

The tragedy of selfishness is that our thoughts, actions, and decisions are dedicated solely to satisfying our needs and desires. Sure, getting our own way feels good. When life goes exactly the way we want it to—the perfect sleepover, the ideal date, the dream vacation—we're on top of the world. Feeling good about ourselves is fine, but when our lives are consumed by the desire to meet our own needs, we will eventually spin out of control.

Selfishness causes us to hurt the people we're closest to. Our minds become consumed with being the smartest, hottest, funniest, and trendiest. We forget that other people have feelings and dreams, and we rarely stop to think about the well-being of those around us. When we are addicted to getting our own way, we do stupid things like these:

thinking we're better than everyone we know

being rude and overly critical

focusing too much on how we look

obsessing about having every hair in place

cutting other people down to feel better about ourselves

unleashing our anger on anyone who points out our flaws

refusing to work on a team

ignoring our friends' pain

Worst of all, we use nagging, gossip, backbiting, and envy to destroy other girls around us who might be threats to our place. Rather than using our words to build up and encourage others, we use our tongues as swords that cut deep gashes in our friends' hearts. And we don't really care.

> If you live life as a selfish person you will not succeed…
> If you live life as a loving person you will.
> **ANNA PEI**

Getting to Know Selfish Sarah

"Well, what's next?" My girlfriends and I were just finishing up lunch at Panera Bread, one of my favorite restaurants. A beautiful spring afternoon with a million possibilities awaited us.

"Gym?" Kristi suggested.

"Mall?" Jacki piped up.

"Park? For a nice nap in the sun," Kate threw in.

"Studying?" I jokingly threw out. A universal groan swept across the table.

"Oh! Oh!" Sarah nearly knocked the table over with her excitement. "Movie. Definitely movie…*New Moon* is still at the theater! C'mon girls, let's go." Sarah jolted out of her seat.

"Sarah, *New Moon* is a good movie, but haven't we already seen it…like, what, three times?"

"Uh, yeah. Which is *why* we should go see it," Sarah retorted. "I mean, *duh*—ten dollars is a small price to pay to see Edward Cullen again! C'mon Megan, you *know* you want to! *Pleeease*?" Sarah playfully jerked my chair.

"But it's a beautiful afternoon out," Kristi jumped in. "I kinda like Kate's idea. You guys wanna relax at the park and get a little sun? We could go to *New Moon* tonight, Sarah."

It sounded like a good compromise to me, but Sarah didn't think so. "But, but…" she whined, "I don't wanna go the park. It'll be muddy. And hot. And besides…lazing around in the grass and doing nothing all day… or gazing into Edward Cullen's eyes with popcorn and Cokes in the *cool* theatre." Now Sarah's voice was tinged with sarcasm. "Hmm…lemme see. Hard choice. Really hard."

When the rest of us still didn't buy into Sarah's idea, she exploded. "Why does it always have to be about what *you* want to do? I'm outta here."

Who knew a perfectly beautiful afternoon could erupt into an argument so quickly? Sarah seemed like a great girl, but when she didn't get her way, she was a volcano—over a silly movie, for heaven's sake! In Sarah's mind, anyone who didn't go along with her way was clearly selfish. Not the best way to make friends, huh?

Welcome to the world of Selfish Sarah. Have you ever had a friend who always has to be in control? Who pouts and whines if she doesn't get her way? Who complains so much she makes life miserable for everyone else?

Sure, we all like being in the limelight. It's fun. It's exciting. But a girl like Selfish Sarah flips out if she's not number one. If she's not calling the shots, selfish Sarah will tear her friends down like crazy. She can be mean, obsessive, manipulative, and heartless.

Every day, you and I are tempted by the desire to live for ourselves. We can feel as if we always have to be right. We can become desperate for control. We can be rude and manipulative. We can cut down our friends just to feel better about ourselves.

We girls can easily forget that *life is not all about us*.

So what's the big deal about selfishness? After all, don't we need to take care of ourselves? To be confident in who we are as young women? To feel beautiful and sexy? To stand up for ourselves?

GIRLS LIKE YOU AND ME HAD THIS TO SAY ABOUT SELFISHNESS...

"Being the center of attention is fun once in a while, but selfishness is the fastest way to destroy your friendships. Nobody wants to hang out with a snob!"
—MARYBETH

"If your life is all about you, you'll live life alone. If you're absorbed with your own world, your world will stay very, very small. Only by listening and caring can we build true friendships."
—SARAH

"If your life is just about getting what you want, you'll end up empty and alone. Selfishness never satisfies, but I'm learning that there is great joy in sharing my life with others."
—LIZ

"I'm learning that I'm not the center of the world. When I have bad days, I try to focus on how I can brighten someone else's day."
—JENNI

"It's natural to be concerned about my life and what I want to do. I have to ask God every day to help me see people the way He does. Really caring about the people around me isn't something I can do on my own."
—AMY

Every girl loves a good comfy T-shirt—and the opportunity to express her own personality! Shopping for some new spring tees recently, my girlfriends and I were a bit surprised by some of the lines that girls proudly wear:

I Love Me

I'm Your After Party

I Am Fashion

You're Just Jealous

Your Boyfriend Is Tweeting Me

All Eyes on Me

I Want It All and I Want It Now

I Recycle Boys

Proud to Be a Violent Sensual Sensitive Girl

Apparently, we girls know how to get what we want. We know how to strut our stuff and use our clothes, our bodies, and our personalities to grab the center of attention. At the core of who we are, every girl is self-absorbed.

We want our way. A lot of us girls live in a small little world, a world all about *me*. Whether we're deciding which movie to watch, what we're having for dinner, or who gets the right of way at the stop sign, the answer will be whatever is best for *me*.

But our desire to be number one can drive us girls to do crazy, mean, and hurtful things. When life is all about having our own way, we don't care what happens to the people around us. So we backbite, manipulate, and walk all over our friends just to make it to the top.

In fact, *Newsweek* reports shocking stories of girls as young as nine years old punching, stabbing, pulling out hair, smashing bottles over classmates' heads, and victimizing other people.[1] In recent years, girls are becoming more violent, and their two most likely targets are peers and family members.

Why do we girls fight? In the heat of the moment, when tempers flare and cruel words fly, we fight to gain status. We want to crush anybody who gets in our way, to get back at other girls, to get even. Girls often fight because of...

a guy

a damaged social standing

gossip and rumors

feeling excluded

being ostracized

"We're rude and we're mean," psychologist Frank Farley observed. "There's road rage, cellphone rage, checkout rage, bike rage, sports rage, parking rage, rail rage, bank rage, roller rage, boat rage, desk rage, car alarm rage, and drivers who even honk at people on crutches!"[2]

A selfish girl is focused on one thing—herself. Forget the girls around her who are hurting. Forget the people who are lonely and just need a friend. Many of us girls live this way. Whether consciously or not, we continually put our own interests, desires, and needs above caring about other people.

We don't even have to learn how to do this. Unfortunately, selfishness is natural. Just like our DNA, it's built into the makeup of who we are. We were all born with sinful hearts, so we easily get consumed with our own little lives, forgetting that we are not the only people in the world.

In our selfishness, we look past other people's pain. We fail to realize that other people have needs, desires, and dreams too. And amazingly, many of us simply don't care to change.

"This is just who I am," we say. "Get over it."

But regardless of how often we get our way, a life lived for self is never satisfying. Sure, it may be fun, but it won't really make us happy. God's heart for His girls is for a life way bigger than ourselves.

Selfish Sarah and You

"Why does it always have to be about what *you* want to do? I'm outta here." As Sarah criticized her friends as selfish, she was totally blind to the fact that her life was all about her. What about you? Does Sarah's story sound a bit familiar? Think you might be too focused on yourself? Take a few minutes to think about these questions and write out your responses.

1. Do I make decisions based on what I can get or what I can give?

2. How do I spend my free time and money? On just eating out, going to movies, and shopping?

3. When was the last time I volunteered my time or money to help someone in need?

4. How do I feel when I don't receive attention or affirmation?

5. How important is it for me to be in control and have things done my way?

6. Does my attitude, body language, and fashion style shout, "look at me"?

7. When I don't get what I want, do I get irritated and angry?

8. When I'm hanging out with friends, does the conversation center around me?

9. When other people tell me about their problems, do I take time to truly care and listen, or do I talk about my own problems?

10. Do I go out of my way to help other people without expecting anything in return?

11. Do I share with others, or is my stuff simply *my* stuff?

How did you do? You may never have considered how much of your life is dedicated to yourself. But don't despair—the good news is that Selfish Sarah and you and I are not doomed to lives of drama and insanity.

You don't have to be desperate for other people's attention and affirmation. You can learn to care about your friends and stop using them. You can step outside of your little world and look for ways to help and encourage those around you. You don't have to shout, "Look at me!" to be beautiful. You can be confident in being yourself rather than trying to look like a Hollywood model.

> If you wish to travel far and fast, travel light. Take off all your envies, jealousies, unforgiveness, selfishness and fears.
> **GLENN CLARK**

Have you ever hurt someone you really cared about without even knowing it? In the heat of the moment, all you could think about was proving your point, getting your way, and being right. And you stomped all over the heart of a friend you love.

If each of us walks around thinking we are the center of our own universe, well, that's a whole lot of universes! A whole lot of worlds that are bound to collide. Not a pretty picture.

People once believed that the earth had to be the center of the universe because it's where we humans live. Turns out we were wrong. The earth is about 93 million miles away from the sun, and it's such a small planet that you could fit 1,300,000 earths inside the sun. And the sun is just one of the smaller stars of trillions out there.

I don't know about you, but all those numbers make my head spin. I may not know a lot, but I do know that compared to the hugeness of the universe that God created, you and I are pretty insignificant. Drops in a bucket. Specks of sand.

"'To whom will you compare me? Or who is my equal?' says the Holy One. 'Lift your eyes and look to the heavens'" (Isaiah 40:25 NIV). God created every single star and calls each one by name. Wow.

Amazingly, this same God who is so big and incomprehensible also tells us that "nothing—nothing living or dead, angelic or demonic, today or tomorrow, high or low, thinkable or unthinkable—absolutely nothing can get between us and God's love" (Romans 8:39). When you and I start to grapple with how big our God is and how small and petty our lives are, we can only say what David did: "I look at my micro-self and wonder, why do you bother with us? Why take a second look our way?" (Psalm 8:4).

When we look at it this way, selfishness is not just bad, it's really bad. When you and I live as if life were all about us, we deny the reality of Jesus as King and Leader over the entire universe and over our individual lives. It's as if we're saying to God, "Okay, so I know You made everything. I know You're the One who holds every cell together, makes my heart beat, and offers me salvation. I know all that...I just think that *my way* is the better way."

Sound ridiculous? It is.

When you and I fail to get God's bigness and the smallness of our own lives, we can become consumed with our own desires and cravings. And when our lives are dedicated to getting what we want, we are without a doubt headed for trouble. No amount of money, popularity, or success can ultimately fulfill the deep longings of our souls.

In the moment, doing things our own way sounds so good. Looking out for ourselves feels natural. Flirting so we can get guys' attention, turning heads, being the best, fighting our way to the top...they all seem so logical, so right.

But deep within our hearts, you and I long to live for something bigger than the drama we create. Deep inside, deeper than our fleeting, selfish desires, we wonder, *Who am I? Why am I here? And what is life really all about?*

Dealing with our selfish, girlish hearts is not just a matter of trying harder. In fact, you and I aren't strong enough on our own to say no to self and yes to God. Simply following rules or getting perfect scores is not the point. The key is to submit our selfish hearts to God and realize that He is our life. God is so spectacular, so incredibly delightful and fulfilling, that a me-centered life pales in comparison.

But Megan, you might be thinking, *I like my life right now. I'm popular. I'm in control. Why would I want to give that up?* Good question. Here's a response from the Bible:

> The person who plants selfishness, ignoring the needs of others—ignoring God!—harvests a crop of weeds. All he'll have to show for his life is weeds! But the one who plants in response to God, letting God's Spirit do the growth work in him, harvests a crop of real life, eternal life (Galatians 6:7-8).

Weeds aren't of much value at all. They taste gross. They choke out healthy grass. They're at the mercy of the weed whacker.

Being in the spotlight may be fun for a moment, but a self-centered life is ultimately meaningless, empty, hollow, and unsatisfying. Sure, you and I may win lots of temporary friends, snag hot guys, and become the most popular girls in school, but at the end of the day, when we take off our makeup, let down our hair, and collapse into bed exhausted, will any of it really matter? Will our hearts be truly satisfied?

Not in the long run.

The Bible challenges us, "Let every detail in your lives—words, actions, whatever—be done in the name of the Master, Jesus, thanking God the Father every step of the way" (Colossians 3:17).

Girls, *this* is what life is all about! *This* is what selfishness blinds us from. *This* is why we exist. *This* is our destiny.

Your Ticket Out

We girls can be selfish for several reasons.

- We think that getting our way is what life is all about. But when situations spin out of our control, we freak out.

- We define ourselves by our ability to turn heads and get attention. So when we're not number one in the room, we use desperate means to get attention.

- We feel insecure in ourselves, and cutting others down makes us feel more confident. That's why we belittle and discredit anybody who seems like competition.

So what's a girl to do? To truly live as God's girl, you and I must intentionally choose to fight selfishness. The Bible puts it this way:

> Think of yourselves the way Christ Jesus thought of himself. He had equal status with God but didn't think so much of himself that he had to cling to the advantages of that status no matter what. Not at all. When the time came, he set aside the privileges of deity and took on the status of a slave, became human!…He didn't claim special privileges. Instead, he lived a selfless, obedient life and then died a selfless, obedient death—and the worst kind of death at that: a crucifixion (Philippians 2:5-8).

If you and I want to be like Jesus, we have to embrace a lifestyle about more than ourselves. Rather than demanding things from God and other people, God's girl looks for little ways to bless and encourage the people God brings across her path.

Rather than focusing on getting, she focuses on giving, caring, listening, and loving.

What does an unselfish girl look like? Look in the dictionary, and you'll find that the opposite of selfish is generous, giving, considerate, kind, patient…and the list goes on. The unselfish girl chooses to break the "me" bubble, not just because it's a good thing to do, but because she sees something way better and way more satisfying to live for than her own pettiness.

So how can you and I break free from selfishness to live as God's girl?

Take Your Selfish Heart to God

We will never be able to handle our own selfishness on our own strength. Honestly, a lot of times, I don't even know I'm being selfish in the moment. It just happens. But good news! "God is greater than our worried hearts and knows more about us than we do ourselves" (1 John 3:20).

Stop and think about it. Before you and I breathed our first breath, God knew every single selfish thought we would ever think and every cutting remark we would make. He knew about every time we would be rude, mean, and heartless. Talking to God, King David exclaims, "You know everything I'm going to say before I start the first sentence" (Psalm 139:4).

God *knows* you and me. Our selfish hearts and thoughts and words and actions don't surprise Him. And only He has the power to help you overcome the "me first" monster. So go to God. Right here, right now. Don't hold back. Don't be shy. Don't try to hide. Just be real.

Ask God to show you the selfishness of your own heart. Ask Him to give you His love and patience for other people rather than the irritation you feel.

Pay Attention to Your Words

Words hold the power to bring great joy or to hurt like crazy, depending on the way we use them. You and I might not walk around with a knife carefully concealed, but the things we say can cut deep, leaving wounds that will take years to heal. God puts it really simply: "Watch the way you talk. Let nothing foul or dirty come out of your mouth. Say only what helps, each word a gift" (Ephesians 4:29).

That means we need to *think* before we lash out in anger and frustration. It means caring about other people instead of venting by stomping all over other people's feelings. You and your friends may never beat up somebody else physically, but "if you keep on biting and devouring each other, watch out or you will be destroyed by each other" (Galatians 5:14 NIV).

Treasure People Instead of Using Them

If we girls really care about other people, we won't use them to get what we want. Instead, we'll want what is best for them. Being manipulative and self-absorbed comes naturally, but true friendship requires the hard work of caring about other people more than yourself.

> Agree with each other, love each other, be deep-spirited friends. Don't push your way to the front; don't sweet-talk your way to the top. Put yourself aside, and help others get ahead. Don't be obsessed with getting your own advantage. Forget yourselves long enough to lend a helping hand (Philippians 2:2-4).

Straightforward? *Yeah.* Hard? *You bet!* Wanting to get ahead is natural. Helping other people get ahead? *Not easy.* But think about it. Every single person we meet is a unique and precious creation of God. Do you really want to be messing around with God's treasures?

Not me.

Intentionally Invest Yourself in Others

Choose to step outside of your little world and look for the needs of other people around you. Do it even if you don't feel like it. Left to myself, I know that my life would become one big crazy contest to get what I want. Maybe you can relate.

But don't get overwhelmed. We can step outside of the "top girl" mentality and begin to see people like God does. Here are a few ideas to get you started:

Send your friends encouraging texts or Facebook messages.

Bake cookies for a neighbor or teacher.

Wash the dishes or fold the laundry for your mom.

Volunteer in your community or church.

Do a random act of kindness without expecting anything in return.

One of the most powerful ways to begin developing an unselfish heart is to give—and not just money. Always be on the lookout for creative ways to invest your time, energy, and focus in helping other people out.

In the Word

If you're serious about living this new resurrection life with

Christ, act like it. Pursue the things over which Christ presides. Don't shuffle along, eyes to the ground, absorbed with the things right in front of you. Look up, and be alert to what is going on around Christ—that's where the action is. See things from his perspective" (Colossians 3:1-2).

This passage cuts right to the heart of every girl's struggle with selfishness. Becoming totally absorbed with our own plans and dreams is like shuffling along with our eyes on the ground. Talk about narrow-minded. Bo-ring! And downright pitiful, huh? What girl in her right mind would choose that kind of life?

Take a second look at Colossians 3. Where's the action? The adventure? The fulfillment? *Where God is*. The apostle Paul goes on to say, "Your old life is dead. Your new life, which is your real life—even though invisible to spectators—is with Christ in God. He is your life" (verse 3).

Choosing to follow Jesus is not just about praying a prayer or avoiding certain attitudes and behaviors. When we give our lives to God, He begins a full-scale overhaul of our hearts, chipping away at our ugly self-centeredness and reshaping us to be like Jesus.

That doesn't mean our selfish impulses magically disappear the instant we surrender to God. But when you and I give our lives to Jesus, He begins opening our eyes to the real nastiness of our pride and self-centeredness. Rather than thinking, *Oh well, that's just who I am*, God's girl has the power of the Holy Spirit to control her selfish impulses and not allow them to control her.

Sound easy? No way. The Bible uses images of war, fighting, and killing our selfish desires, armed with the unshakable truth of our new life in Jesus. Paul continues in Colossians 3 with this:

That means killing off everything connected with that way of death: sexual promiscuity, impurity, lust, doing whatever you feel like whenever you feel like it, and grabbing whatever attracts your fancy. That's a life shaped by things and feelings instead of by God (Colossians 3:5).

God's girl knows who she is, and she chooses to fight selfishness every single day from the moment she wakes up till she falls asleep at night.

Those who do not hate their own selfishness and who regard themselves as more important than the rest of the world are blind because the truth lies elsewhere.

BLAISE PASCAL

Smart Girls Remember...

- A selfish life is small, measly, and pitiful.
- Selfishness is the natural condition of every girl's heart, but if you live your life only to make yourself happy, you'll always be disappointed.
- When you cut other people down to make yourself feel better, you're crushing the hearts of God's precious children so you can have an ego trip.
- Selfishness is really self-worship. It robs God of the glory and worship He deserves.
- Really *caring* about other people is impossible without the strength of God in your heart.

Father God,

I have such a difficult time caring about other people. Sometimes I just get carried away by what I want! God, help me to see how small and meaningless my self-centered lifestyle is. Open my eyes to something bigger to live for—show me Your heart. Give me Your love for the people around me. Help me to want to worship You alone, God, not me. You deserve all the glory for Yourself. I want to share Your awesomeness with the whole world!

Amen.

Addicted to Approval

*I have this desire to prove something to somebody...I can't be
satisfied with pleasing myself: I have to please other people.*

PAT TRAVERS

In the movie *Sydney White*, Sydney is a confident yet conflicted girl. She
is accepted by the college she hoped to attend and pledges to the prestigious Phi Kappa Nu sorority, just as her mom had done years earlier.
The Kappas are the talk of the campus, and hundreds of girls would *die*
to be in Sydney's spot.

Enter the Phi Kappa Nu girls, struttin' their stuff. They're perfectly put
together, blond, skinny, snobby, prissy, and downright mean. The movie
trailer hints at what's about to happen: "On a campus full of wannabes,
Sydney White was an original. But in a house where everyone is trying to
fit in, it's not always good to stand out."

Raised by her dad, Sydney is strong and confident, and she makes no
bones about who she is. Much to her dismay, Sydney just doesn't fit into
the superficial, materialistic lifestyle. "I'm sorry," she tells Rachel Witch-
burn, the leader of the Kappas. "I'm still learning to speak priss."

Life is all about stuff for Rachel and her posse, who seem to care more
about Prada, Gucci, and Chanel than anything else. And Sydney is faced
with a tough decision: *Do I change myself? Dye my hair blond? Starve myself
thin? Put on the emerald and pearl cardigan? Buy a Gucci bag? Slip on the
heels? Turn up my nose at everyone else? Compete for number one on the "Hot
or Not" website?*

Tough call. Some girls will do crazy things just to fit in. But for Sydney,
it's just not worth it. "You will never be a Kappa," Rachel cuts. But amazingly, being dismissed from the Kappas doesn't crush Sydney's world.

Not even close.

Stepping back from the popular crowd, Sydney chooses to be who she is. Proudly. Rather than bemoaning the Kappa's rejection, Sydney throws herself into helping out the nerds and the dorks—the social outcasts whom the Kappa girls are trying to stomp out.

And at the end of the day, Sydney doesn't miss the Kappas one bit. She discovers that the uncool, unpopular guys and girls may be the best friends a girl could ask for.

If only you and I could be so confident facing our own Kappas! Okay, maybe we're not up against a sorority, but be honest. We girls tend to care way too much about what other people think.

From elementary school on, life easily becomes about hanging with the in crowd. But when our lives become obsessed with making other people happy—by what we wear, what we say, or what we do—we put ourselves in bondage. We become slaves of whatever is currently the rage. And we lose our identity.

In this chapter, we're going to dive into people-pleasing and get to the bottom of the addiction many of us girls have for approval. Looking at the influence our friends hold over our lives, we're going to rediscover the core of our unchanging identity in God Himself—not in fashion, not in other people, not in Hollywood, and not in GPAs or letters earned in sports. God Himself is the key to who we are.

Defining Approval Addiction

So what does it mean to be a performer? To be bound by the approval of other people? Like a dancer on the stage of life, an approval addict is driven by the overwhelming desire to be liked and accepted by other people. This kind of girl is ambitious, motivated, and even obsessed with praise and applause. She's like an actress on stage. Her every action is motivated by pleasing her audience—her friends, classmates, teachers, coworkers, and family.

Of course, many of us enjoy other people's attention. But approval is the drug of choice for some of us. We *have* to have it. It's almost like we get a high from making other people happy. Some of us will do anything for anybody just to get acceptance and praise.

So what do we do? We change our fashion style, our hairdo, our music, or our lingo just to fit in with the cool crowd. We need to be popular, to be hip, to be in with the latest fashion.

Don't get me wrong—I love fashion. I love dressing up and feeling cute. But think about it. We girls get extreme sometimes. We get so desperate to fit in that we work out obsessively, starve ourselves, or maybe binge and purge to try to get the perfect body.

The tragedy of this performance mentality is that we set aside, devalue, and even begin to hate who we really are because of the pressure we feel to dress and act a certain way—just so we can hang out with the cool crowd. When we're crazy for other people's approval and attention, we often...

  are self-conscious and worried about slipping up

  lack confidence in ourselves

  will do just about anything just to be accepted

  try to dress and act just like our friends

  believe whatever others think

  don't have a clue who we are apart from the group

  get depressed when we're not noticed or the center of attention

  avoid uncool people to protect our reputation

In this difficult kind of life, we ultimately lose who we are in our attempts to become the ever-elusive perfect girl. We let other people tell us who we are and what our lives will be about. But that right belongs solely to God.

Performing for an audience is exhausting. That's why most Broadway shows are only a few hours long. Imagine a dancer or actress performing nonstop for days, weeks, months...Talk about a formula for disaster! Sound insane? It is! But that's exactly what we girls do when we live to make other people happy.

> Be who you are and say what you feel because those who mind don't matter and those who matter don't mind.
> **DR. SEUSS**

Getting to Know Approval-Addict Amy

"So how's life? What's goin' on?" Amy asked me as we stuffed down a quick lunch between classes.

How's life? "Well," I quipped, "It'd be great if it wasn't for chemistry. I mean, I know I gotta know this stuff if I want to go to med school, but sometimes I just wanna burn my book and be done with it. You know?"

"Especially on test week!" Amy agreed, laughing.

"It's like I study for hours and hours, and I'm just not getting it."

"Hmm...would it help you if we sat down and talked through it? Went over some problems?" Amy suggested. "I may be a little rusty, but I did really enjoy that class."

"But...don't you have your calc test coming up?" I asked her as we grabbed our backpacks. "I mean, I don't want to take you away from that."

Amy's phone rang. "Hold on." She smiled. "Hey Kate! What's up?... You what?...Oh, man. Where you at?...Okay, hold on. I'll be right there... Love ya, girl. Bye."

"I gotta run and pick Kate up. Her car won't start, and she has class. Oh—my calc test? Ah, not a biggie. I can study for that later. Seriously though. Library. Four o'clock. I'll meet you there."

Whew. Am I ever grateful for a friend like Amy! For nearly two hours, Amy walked me through the steps of calculating chemical formulas. I probably learned more chemistry that afternoon than I had all semester!

I love Amy. Whenever I hang out with her, she makes me feel like I'm the only person in the room. Regardless of how much homework she has to do or what stresses are on her mind, she doesn't hesitate for a second to set it aside just to help me.

But sometimes I worry about her. Amy is *always* helping people out. Later that night, I bumped into her at Starbucks with our friend Sarah, who'd just broken up with her boyfriend. Overhearing their conversation as I stood in line, I saw Amy's genuine concern for Sarah. She really cared.

Back in the dorm, my friend Josie was bubbling with excitement. "Come see my new dress! Amy helped me pick it out today. You know, I'm not the best at fashion, but Amy—man, does she have an eye for style! I love that girl!"

Oh, Amy. Chemistry tutor, taxi service, boyfriend advisor, fashion consultant, marriage counselor, *and* a premed student? Sometimes I think Amy's a superwoman in disguise.

Not!

Going to brush my teeth before bed that night, I ran into Amy again. She was sitting in the hall with her calc book and a big pack of Oreos, talking on the phone. "Mom, it's gonna be okay. I'm sure Dad didn't mean what he said. Don't worry. Just hang in there. I'll come home this weekend. I promise...Okay, love you, Mom. Bye."

"Amy, what are you doing? Go to sleep, girl," I mumbled.

"Sleep? Ha. Sleep's overrated. Just talking to my mom. She and Dad got in a fight again..." Amy sighed. "Now for some good ol' calc. Gotta get this done. If I don't get an A, my dad will kill me." Amy grabbed another Oreo and stuck her earbuds in.

At two a.m., I stumbled to the bathroom and walked in on Amy kneeling over the toilet and gagging.

"Amy? Are you okay?"

Tears streaming down her face, Amy turned away from me. "Uhhh... I'm sorry, Megan. I just...I just...life is...uuuhhh. I can't handle this."

"Amy, c'mere." I grabbed Amy's hand and pulled her up into a hug. "It's okay. Relax."

"But Megan, I can't," she sobbed. "The stress. The pressure...it's too much. I want to be strong. To be there for other people, but then I go do something like *this*. I eat when I'm stressed, and then I feel so fat, and I...I just have to get it out. I'm such a failure. If anybody finds out, my life is over."

Until that night, I'd never seen Amy desperate before, but sitting on the bathroom floor at two a.m., she was falling apart. Amy—one of the kindest, strongest, godliest girls I know—was deathly afraid of what other people would think of her.

Amy was afraid to be herself, to let people know about her problems. Amy couldn't say no to anybody. Every moment was a desperate dance to try to keep everybody happy. Amy lived for the approval of her friends, her mom, and her dad. Whatever it took, she was willing to do...all just to hear them say "Thank you" and "You're such a good friend" and "I know I can always count on you."

GIRLS LIKE YOU AND ME HAD THIS TO SAY ABOUT LIVING FOR APPROVAL...

"I think I've missed out on a lot because I tend to worry too much about what other people think of me. I'm learning that most of them really don't care about every little mistake I make."
—PEGGY

"When you are sad, don't be afraid to show it! Cry! I wish someone would have told me that I didn't always have to put on a show like it was all okay...and that someone would have told me that I was allowed to be hurt. Don't act like you have everything together—if you need help, *find it!*"
—JENNA

"For years, I felt like everyone but me had a manual for life. No one knew how I felt because I was a cheerleader, I was outgoing, and I had a lot of friends. I just wish someone had told me before that everyone feels the same way I do sometimes."
—TRACY

"Keep in touch with your friends! Don't worry about the latest fashions. Wear what makes you feel comfortable and maintain your self-respect and honor. Be true to yourself. And don't try to please everyone around you. That's insane. And impossible."
—SAMMIE

"If I could talk to teenage girls, I would want to impress upon them how much God loves them as they are...pimples and all! I would want to encourage them to keep going and to find their hope in God and not in friends or boys or the future."
—MICHELLE

Outside, Amy was smiling and happy. But inside, the drive for approval was killing her.

We all want to be loved, accepted, and appreciated. So many of us girls go through life with one goal: to make other people happy. We start to believe lies like these:

> My identity is defined by the way other people see me.
>
> My worth is based on what I do.
>
> I need to do whatever is necessary to make other people happy.
>
> I can never disappoint anyone or fail at anything.
>
> I'm stuck—this is how I am and I can never change.

Regardless of how hard we try or how good our intentions are, if we live to make our parents or our teachers or our boyfriends or our friends happy, we will always be disappointed. Every single time.

Face it. Try as we might, we can't make everybody happy. There are way too many people out there, and there's not nearly enough time! And the tragic thing is, when we're addicted to other people's approval, we wear ourselves out trying to prove that we're smart enough and pretty enough to be perfect. We waste our lives trying to prove ourselves, strutting our stuff, and convincing other people that we're "all that."

"Practically perfect in every way" may work for a fairy-tale character like Mary Poppins, but in real life, if we try to have perfect grades, the perfect body, perfect makeup, and perfect hair, we'll eventually crash and burn. We can kill ourselves trying, but we'll never get there.

Nearly every girl I know struggles with her body image. I know I do sometimes! We can easily buy into the thin-is-in lie. It's promoted everywhere—in TV shows and movies, books and magazines, billboards and commercials. And if the way we spend money says anything, a lot of us believe we have to fit a certain cookie-cutter mold. Women in America spend $7 billion on cosmetics every year. But aside from the usual mascara, blush, and lipstick, a lot of us girls are resorting to surgery in our search for perfection. Look how much we're spending on these cosmetic surgeries:

> breast augmentation ($1.5 billion per year)
>
> lipoplasty ($1.3 billion)
>
> eyelid surgery ($684 million)

tummy tucks ($992 million)

breast reduction ($829 million)[1]

American girls are driven to meet an unrealistic standard of beauty. We think that having the perfect body will win us love and approval. We fall for this lie, forgetting that the airbrushed advertisements featuring skimpily clad women aren't based on reality. Or good health.

Think about it. The average woman is five feet four and weighs 140 pounds, but the average model is 5 feet 11 inches and weighs 117 pounds—thinner than 98 percent of women in America![2]

The truth is, more than half of us girls would rather be run over by a truck than be fat. And two-thirds of us would rather be mean or stupid than have a less than perfect body.[3] Sound extreme? I had to laugh when I discovered these statistics, but for a lot of us girls, it's reality.

I recently read that more than half of all teenage girls are using unhealthy ways of losing weight, like fasting, smoking, vomiting, or consuming laxatives, and that 90 percent of girls with eating disorders are between 12 and 25 years old. Wow, what does that say about our self-image?

When we're working so hard trying to be perfect, trying to make everybody happy, we can forget who we really are. The dance requires all our attention. The spotlight leaves us sweaty and exhausted. Miss a step, and it's all over. Approval addicts act as if failure isn't an option, and when they do fall (as we all do), it's almost like the end of the world. No second chances, no springing back. When we can't make other people happy, we tend to think life is no longer worth living. In fact, one in eight teens struggle with depression, and teen girls are twice as likely to be depressed as guys.[4]

Somewhere along the line, you and I start basing our self-worth on our bodies, our achievements, our ability to get and keep other people's attention, our status, and our popularity. And when we don't measure up, life can feel miserable.

A freckle makes us freak out. A social slip-up causes us to withdraw from our friends. An F on a test plunges us into huge depression. A swing and a miss in softball or in life makes us seriously question whether life is worth living. We're deathly afraid of messing up, and sometimes we'd rather die than face a failure. Fear becomes a huge factor—fear of rejection, fear of failure, fear of not fitting in, fear of not being loved by other people.

Approval-Addict Amy and You

"I'm such a failure. If anybody finds out, my life is over." Amy's desperate words erupted from the heart of a young woman whose desire to fit in led to a never-ending struggle to make people happy. But the performance was eating away at her time, her health, and her identity. Every apparently selfless act was an attempt to drown out the voice screaming inside, *You're not good enough!* Amy wondered if she could ever feel like she was worth something without letting other people walk all over her.

What about you? Does Amy's story sound familiar? Are you living your life to make other people happy? Do you have a hard time saying no? Consider each of these questions and write down a response to each one.

1. Am I a people pleaser? Do I *need* to make other people happy?

2. Do I constantly seek other people's opinions? Do I live for compliments?

3. Is it hard for me to make decisions on my own?

4. Do I try to impress others with the way I dress, the way I talk, and what I accomplish?

5. Is fitting in more important for me than having strong values and morals?

6. Do I worry a lot about what other people think about me?

7. When I am criticized or fail to meet other people's expectations, how do I respond?

8. What lengths will I go to in order to make someone else happy? Do I tend to burn myself out and go to extremes?

9. Do I often wonder if I'm good enough, smart enough, or beautiful enough?

10. Do I constantly compare myself to other people?

Was this exercise helpful? Did you discover any red flags? You don't have to live in fear of what other people think of you. You can learn to be the confident woman God made you to be. You can be free to be yourself.

You can learn to make sound and God-honoring decisions. You can set healthy boundaries in your life. You can learn to tell other people no.

It all starts with getting your eyes off yourself—and off of other people too.

> A truly strong person does not need the approval of others any more than a lion needs the approval of sheep.
> **VERNON HOWARD**

Have you ever been tempted to change who you are just to make somebody else happy? Maybe you really liked a hot guy and wanted to snag his attention. Maybe you went to a new school and wanted to fit in with the in crowd. Or maybe you felt obligated to help a friend when you were already pulling your hair out with stress. Somewhere, sometime, you have experienced the sinking feeling of insecurity. *What if I'm not pretty enough to attract him? What if my clothes aren't cool enough for the popular girls? What if I say no and my friend gets mad? Then what?*

A lot of us really are driven by the fear of letting other people down, of not measuring up to their expectations. And so we dance on, despite bruised knees, blistered heels, and bloody toes. We strain our ears and our hearts to hear the applause of our friends, our teachers, our coaches, our family, our boyfriends...

But after the show is over, the lights go out and we are left in the dark. The noise dies away as the crowd disperses into the night, and we are alone. When we live to please others, we feel as if we are only as good as our last dance because the dance defines us.

But we're not really alone. God never leaves, and He is always whispering, *I love you, precious girl. You belong to Me*. He gently wipes away the tears that roll down our tear-stained faces when we're exhausted and can't go on anymore. *Come, love, let's wipe those tears away*. And somehow, in that moment, with Him as our only audience, nothing else matters.

> Lean too much on the approval of others,
> and it becomes a bed of thorns.
> **TEHYI HSIEH**

Your Ticket Out

Why do we become performers?

- We think we're only as good as our last test grade, our last outfit, or our last date. We're desperately afraid of failing, and when we do fail, we think we're worthless.

- We want to be the center of attention. We want to be noticed. We're seduced by the glamour of life in the spotlight. We'll do anything to satisfy our addiction to other people's praise and attention.

- We could never be good enough for our parents, and we've been rejected over and over again by people who should have loved us, so we're absolutely terrified of making anyone mad or letting other people down.

Maybe as you've been reading, you've realized that you can identify with Approval-Addict Amy. In a way, we're all kind of like that. After all, caring about what other people think is just part of being human. In fact, "a good name is more desirable than great riches" (Proverbs 22:1 NIV).

The problem comes when you and I start defining ourselves based on what other people think. But stop for a second and think about it. Is *any* girl out there perfect? In the Bible, God answers that question matter-of-factly:

> There's nobody living right, not even one,
>   nobody who knows the score, nobody alert for God.
> They've all taken the wrong turn;
>   they've all wandered down blind alleys (Romans 3:10).

When we go through life trying to be perfect, trying to make everybody happy, we're doing more than merely stressing ourselves out. We're worshipping ourselves. We live in a culture that is all about doing, accomplishing, and going for the gold, so we naturally think that if we just try hard enough, we can earn approval from our friends, our parents, and even God.

As if we could win God's love with our blood, sweat, and tears! If we buy into this attitude, we are rejecting the gospel. We are saying no to grace because we think our efforts will do what only Jesus' perfect life and atoning death could do. Rather than living in God's grace, many of us are relying on our own strength. And we live as if we have something to prove. We don't! God's favor doesn't come and go. His love and acceptance doesn't depend on what we do any more than the sun rising depends on the direction we're facing!

For a lot of my life, I ran around like a chicken with my head cut off, trying like crazy to be good enough. To make the teams, to keep the rules, to put a smile on God's face with my brilliance. Ha! What a messed-up view of God I had! We are learning to live as God's girls when we accept a new view of God—and of ourselves.

"Christ has set us free to live a free life. So take your stand! Never again let anyone put a harness of slavery on you" (Galatians 5:1). Have you been living in bondage to what other people think? Have you been trying to squish yourself into a cookie-cutter mold of what somebody told you a good girl does?

You don't have to.

But if we don't want to be driven by performance, what's the alternative? The opposite of performing is living in peace. Resting. *Being* instead of *doing*. Not feeling the compulsive need to be center stage all the time. Granted, all of us have plenty of stuff to do. Being motivated is a good thing. But when we live for the dance—the performance, the applause— that's when *doing* becomes an idol. That's when we gradually quit listening to God and start following the voices in the crowd.

The girl who's not an approval addict is free to become the woman God wants her to be and is not bound to constantly strive to make other people happy. So how do we break free?

Be Captivated by the Audience of One

We are constantly enticed by the excitement, the bling, and the stardom that approval brings. That's why the Bible specifically tells us, "Don't compare yourself to others" (Galatians 6:4). Be honest—we all do. *Is she smarter or wittier or prettier than me? Does her bathing suit look better? Is her hair style cuter?*

Natural though these comparisons may be, they are prideful and debilitating. The comparison trap keeps us from becoming the women God wants us to be because all we can think about is getting attention, coming out on top, and being in control.

We forget God's face and God's heart. We forget that nothing we could ever do would change the way God sees us—here and now, just as we are. So we run ourselves ragged working for God and forget to bask in His presence. To just enjoy *being* His girls before we *do* anything.

Learn to Say No

When you and I are living to please other people, we have a hard time saying no to our friends' requests. We're afraid they will think that no really means "I hate you, and I don't want to be your friend."

Huh? That's messed up. Think about it. If you and I always say yes to everybody, we will never know who we are or where we're going. We will be tossed back and forth like a little sailboat in a crazy thunderstorm. And we probably won't accomplish much of anything.

When God custom-knit you together in your mommy's tummy (Psalm 139:13), He made you the way He did for a reason. That means that your personality, your talents, and even your body was specially created in the way that can bring God the most glory.

But I've got news for you: You can't be everybody. And you can't make everybody happy. Try to do it all, and you'll end up strung out, stressed, and without a clue about what *you* even want anymore.

Saying no is not selfish. It's often the healthy thing to do. After all, if you don't learn to set boundaries in your life, you'll fall prey to anything that anybody tells you to do.

Do a Heart Check

Why do you and I do the things we do? The answer probably has to do with the fact that in the moment, we do what is most important to us. Every day, the decisions we make show a snapshot of our hearts' strongest desires.

Our longing as girls to be loved, valued, and affirmed can become extreme and drive us into the desperate dance of approval. But when we try to make everybody happy, we end up making nobody happy.

Remember, we don't exist for the applause of the crowd. Our heavenly Father custom-designed us for one purpose: to bring Him glory. We might think that working really hard and being really busy brings God glory, but that's not necessarily the case. It all depends on the reason *why* we do what we do. For example, the apostle Paul reminds his readers about what did and did not motivate him: "Do you think I speak this strongly in order to manipulate crowds? Or curry favor with God? Or get popular applause? If my goal was popularity, I wouldn't bother being Christ's slave" (Galatians 1:10).

Maybe it's time for a heart check. Ask yourself, *What is my goal? What do I want most?*

Live in Your New Identity

It's easy to define ourselves by our talents, beauty, or success (or the lack thereof), but the thing is, all of these things are temporary. You or I could get in a car accident and be in a wheelchair for the rest of our lives. We could lose our ability to play sports, walk, or even talk!

Then what? If our identity is just wrapped up in our looks, our achievements, and our friends, we'll eventually fall flat on our faces. According to a 2002 study, "The happiest people...pursue personal growth and intimacy; they judge themselves by their own yardsticks, never against what other people do or have."[5]

As a Christ follower, your identity is grounded in God Himself. Your ruler is the Bible, and you can trust what it says. Regardless of what anyone tells you, regardless of how ugly or worthless you may feel, build your identity on truths like these:

> I am God's workmanship (Ephesians 2:10 NIV).
>
> I am free from condemnation (Romans 8:1-2 NIV).
>
> I am Jesus' friend (John 15:15).
>
> I have been redeemed and forgiven of every sin (Colossians 1:13-14 NIV).
>
> I have direct access to God (Hebrews 4:14-16).

Your identity is not wrapped up in what you do, but in who you are—your heart, your character, and your inestimable value to God.

In the Word

"Are you tired?" Jesus asks us. "Come to me."

"Worn out? Come to me."

"Burned out on religion? Come to me."

Living to please other people is exhausting. And it's empty. Regardless of how great the moment or how loud the applause, when it's all over, the people pleaser is still just the world's greatest dancer. Jesus wants us to stop dancing, stop trying to earn His approval, stop making poor decisions, and stop doing things just to please other people. There's no life in that—just mindless drudgery and bondage. Matthew 11:28-30 is worth repeating here:

> Get away with me and you'll recover your life. I'll show you
> how to take a real rest. Walk with me and work with me—
> watch how I do it. Learn the unforced rhythms of grace. I
> won't lay anything heavy or ill-fitting on you. Keep company
> with me and you'll learn to live freely and lightly.

A lot of people shy away from religion because they think it's just a bunch of rules that will keep them from having fun in life. But the truth is that God's way is the only way to really live and be free. Everything that God asks us to do as His girls is for our good—even if it hurts or if we don't want to do it.

But with other people, we don't have that same assurance. Even well-meaning friends can cause us a lot of heartbreak, not to mention the people out there that just want to use us or get something from us.

We girls tend to trust people way too easily. And we don't trust God enough. We don't really *get* God's love. We feel as if it's a give-and-take of some kind, as if God and the people around us are holding their breath, just waiting for us to get our act together.

We get drawn into performing in many different ways. Some of us girls give into peer pressure and compromise sexually just to feel loved by a guy. We ignore people who really need us. We use drugs. We cut. We binge and purge. We do a million things to try to meet the expectations we think people have.

But we never can. Inevitably, our best attempts spiral down into hope-lessness. Regardless of how hard we try, we will always bump into *some-body* who doesn't like us. And we can be okay with that because our goal in life isn't just to be cool or hip or popular. God's girl doesn't live to fit in—she stands out. Confidently. The apostle Paul has this to say about people who need to strut their stuff: "In all this comparing and grading and com-peting, they quite miss the point" (2 Corinthians 10:12).

God's girl knows who she is—a daughter of Jesus—and she doesn't let other people push her around. Sure, she cares about what other people think. I mean, every girl does. But at the end of the day, God's girl can curl up in bed with confidence in the one thing that matters most: God's unconditional love. Paul certainly had that assurance, even when he was in jail! Listen to what he wrote to his friends from his prison cell: "There has never been the slightest doubt in my mind that the God who started this great work in you would keep at it and bring it to a flourishing fin-ish" (Philippians 1:6).

Never the slightest doubt... regardless of how we do on a test, or how many friends we have on Facebook, or how many guys do (or don't) ask us out, or how many points we score in the volleyball game. Here's the deal. Even when God's girl does trip and fall and end up on her face, she gets back up again. Sure, she's aware of the audience, but she's not danc-ing for their approval.

She's dancing *with* God.

And keeping her eyes on His face, she dances—and lives—for Him. She knows that He loves her and smiles at her and bursts with joy simply because she is His girl, not because of how well she can dance.

Wouldn't you just love to stop dancing *for* people and start dancing *with* God? I would.

If you please God, it doesn't matter who you displease. But if you displease God, it doesn't matter who you please.
ANONYMOUS

Smart Girls Remember...

- Living your life to make other people happy will make you shallow and leave you empty. Besides, succeeding is impossible.

- God isn't waiting for you to get your act together. He loves you just the way you are.

- Learn to say no to people, or you will burn out. Neglecting yourself doesn't honor God.

- You will never earn God's favor. The things you do for Him are your gifts of love to Him, not obligations to fulfill.

- Your existence and worth are not based on what you do or fail to do. You are inexpressibly valuable because God created you, He has poured His life into you, and He loves you more than you will ever comprehend.

Hey God,

I'm going to be completely honest with You. I care way too much about what other people think. I'm so sorry, God. I know this must hurt Your heart. I'm kind of addicted to attention from boys. I can't seem to live without other people's approval—especially my friends, and sometimes my parents too. If they're mad at me, I just want to die. But I want to change, God. Please help me. I know that Your approval matters the most, and I want to live my life for You, God. I want to be content with Your smile rather than always relying on other people to make me feel good about myself.

In Jesus' name. Amen.

5

Chained to Insecurity

What if they say I'm no good? What if they say,
"Get outta here, kid. You got no future"?

MARTY IN *BACK TO THE FUTURE*

The Hundred Acre Wood was one of my favorite childhood retreats. On sweltering summer afternoons and snowy winter nights, I loved crawling up in my dad's lap and jumping into the crazy adventures of a small, hunny-addicted golden bear, a big bouncy tiger, and a timid little pink pig.

But of all A.A. Milne's characters, my favorite (without question!) would have to be Eeyore—a bluish gray, sawdust-stuffed donkey whose favorite word is *gloomy*. After all, Eeyore's ramshackle stick house is known as "Eeyore's Gloomy Place: Rather Boggy and Sad." Life's pretty hard for this little ol' grey donkey! Glimpsing the reflection of his face in the stream on his birthday morning, Eeyore can only think of one word.

"Pathetic. That's what it is. Pathetic."

He turned and walked slowly down the stream for twenty yards, splashed across it, and walked slowly back on the other side. Then he looked at himself in the water again.

"As I thought," he said. "No better from this side. But nobody minds. Nobody cares. Pathetic, that's what it is."

There was a crackling noise in the bracken behind him, and out came Pooh.

"Good morning, Eeyore," said Pooh.

"Good morning, Pooh Bear," said Eeyore gloomily. "If it *is* a good morning," he said. "Which I doubt," said he.

77

Whether it's the honeybees, the river, his stick house, or a rainstorm, Eeyore can *always* find something to grumble about. "There's only one rain cloud in the sky…and it's raining on me," Eeyore moans. "Somehow I'm not surprised."[1]

Ever felt like Eeyore? Ever felt as if your life were pathetic? Gloomy? Boring?

I love the character of Eeyore because I can relate. On some days, I wake up, look in the mirror, and think, *Ugh…*

Sure, we don't live in the Hundred Acre Wood, and we might not sleep every night in a ramshackle stick house, but sometimes life can dish up some pretty tough stuff. Stuff that's way worse than a raincloud in the sky.

Maybe your dad walked out. Your boyfriend broke up with you. Your mom got cancer. Your best friend ditched you for a guy. You didn't make the team. You got a bad grade. Maybe you messed around with a guy who said he loved you, only to leave you alone when something better came along.

Whatever it was, it hurt a lot. And maybe it's still hurting. So how do we cope? How do we move on? We can easily get confused and begin to feel insecure. Still, we try to keep things together and may even paste on a smile and pretend we're fine.

But inside? Inside, we hate the way things are and begin to doubt ourselves. We might hate the people who hurt us. Somewhere along the line, we start believing what other people said about us—that life is no good and maybe even that we are worthless, ugly, insignificant, or stupid.

These words run through our mind nonstop. And there's no getting away. What started as an off day can turn into an off week or an off month. And our world can get pretty gloomy.

In this chapter, we're going to dig into the universal problem we girls have with hating ourselves…with thinking our lives are worthless and no good. Together, we're going to consider why we feel this way and rediscover how God sees us as His girls.

Defining Low Self-Esteem

So what is self-image? It's the way we see ourselves and feel about ourselves. It's the way we value ourselves and present ourselves to other people.

Sound kind of abstract? Think about it as if we were given a blank canvas and told to paint a self-portrait. A wide array of colors and a variety of brushes lay at our disposal: the parents brush, the friends brush, the boyfriend brush, the teachers brush, the coaches brush...

The easel sits in a prominent corner of our minds. It's a constant reminder of who we are, or at least who we *think* we are. Day by day, we pick up a brush and paint. Blues, greens, and reds; a touch of brown and some orange...and each brush leaves a slightly different mark.

Sometimes the colors get messy and blur together. The paint gets crusty and our brushes get stiff. Eventually, the breathtaking portrait we had envisioned starts looking like a sad mess. Sure, we all have our down days, but a girl who struggles with low self-esteem (and let's face it—we all do from time to time!) can't shake the nagging feeling of being less than.

We all have bad hair days, get the occasional low grade, and blush through awkward social interactions every once in a while. But when our self-esteem plummets, we feel worthless and believe these embarrassing moments define us. Like Eeyore, a little cloud starts to follow us.

And then what happens? We start thinking, *What does it even matter what I do?* So we give up trying in school. We stop pursuing our dreams. We settle for the first boy who mumbles, "I love you." We let guys abuse us because we don't think we deserve any better. We drink, smoke, use drugs, and hurt ourselves because nobody seems to really care what happens to us.

The tragedy of insecurity is that we forget who we really are. Our feelings of self-hatred can lead us into a whole lot of pain and heartbreak. We beat ourselves up for no reason, and every little mistake confirms our feelings of worthlessness. When we go through life this way, we often...

> aren't happy or content with the way God made us
>
> set low standards for ourselves
>
> can't believe God would ever love losers like us
>
> compare ourselves with other girls and feel threatened by them
>
> copy other people's hairstyle, fashion, and lingo to try and fit in
>
> act recklessly because we really don't care what happens to us

> hide behind a pasted-on smile and a put-together facade
>
> thrive on other people's pity and have a false sense of humility
>
> are overly vulnerable, especially with guys

We start believing that we're not worth anything, that we could never be normal, that we're so messed up that no one could ever really love us. So we don't respect ourselves. We let people walk all over us. Some of us stop caring and even give up on our dreams.

Getting to Know No-Good Nikki

"Uhhhh…my life is just the pits," Nikki moaned, crumpling her history test as we walked down the hall. "Another F. I am *so* stupid."

As we headed to the locker room to get ready for PE, Nikki continued, "Well, there goes hanging out with Jake on Friday night. Mom said if I didn't pass my tests this week, she'd ground me. Great. Just great. Which means Jake will probably sneak out with Katie. Uh. I hate that boy sometimes."

"If he's cheating on you, why don't you break up with him?" I asked her. "I mean, if he's gonna mess around with other girls while he says he's with you…that's just messed up."

"You don't understand, Megan. You have a lot going for you, but Jake is all I have. He's the only one who really cares about me. Sure, maybe he gets weird sometimes, but hey, at least he doesn't treat me like an outcast like a lot of other people do."

"But Nikki, Jake isn't who you are. If he really cares about you, he'll respect you. And if not…well, why settle?"

Nikki was the new girl at school. Her family moved to the area just after her mom and dad got divorced, and I could tell Nikki was having a hard time with it. Making friends wasn't easy for Nikki. She lived in her own world. When I invited Nikki over to spend the night, she was surprised. "Why would you wanna hang out with me?"

It took a little convincing, but Nikki finally agreed, and we had a great time. After that, Nikki quickly latched on to me. In fact, as weird as this may seem, she actually started trying to copy me—same haircut, same purse, same music.

GIRLS LIKE YOU AND ME HAD THIS TO SAY ABOUT INSECURITY...

"Growing up, I was very shy, had few friends, and was a real tomboy. I wanted to belong to a group, any group. I had very little confidence."
—MARIE

"Be confident in who God made you to be because that is exactly how He designed you and He loves you that way."
—JAIMIE

"You don't have to be what the world and your peers tell you to be. I wish I would have believed that I was beautiful in my own skin when I was younger."
—LESLIE

"My parents were very critical, and I grew up hearing how I could improve. No matter how hard I tried, I couldn't be good enough. But God's not like that! He loves us unconditionally."
—JESSICA

"For years I didn't believe God loved me because I thought He was dissatisfied with me."
—LAUREN

"Everyone is made uniquely, and *everyone* is beautiful in her own way. I just took a while to see and believe this."
—MARYANN

But I ached as I watched my new friend beat herself up all the time. Nikki was always calling herself ugly or fat or dumb. She seemed to thrive on other people's pity. She was the kind of girl who didn't think she was worth anything.

Sure, we all have rough days, but Nikki seemed convinced that *loser* was written on her forehead in big black letters. Ever felt like that? Do you ever feel as if God somehow messed up when He made you? That you're somehow inferior to every other kid in your school? Do you ever hate yourself?

As girls, we all struggle with being down on ourselves sometimes. If we aren't careful, though, our failures can become big, ugly monsters that haunt us all the time. Like Nikki, we can start believing lies about who we are. Our insecurity often drives us to do anything just to feel loved.

So what's the big deal about insecurity? Why do we as girls tend to be so hard on ourselves? Research shows that girls' self-esteem peaks when we're about nine years old and then takes a nosedive.[2]

On our journey from childhood to womanhood, a lot changes—and I'm not just talking about our bodies! As teenage girls, we start to care a lot more about what other people think and say about us than we did as little kids. And whether we realize it or not, what our parents and coaches and friends and boyfriends say *shapes* the way we see ourselves. In fact, powerful voices are all around us:

- advertisements, movies, and TV shows that glamorize images that are picture-perfect
- parents (especially dads) who have unrealistic expectations, who are disinterested, or who abuse us
- female role models with low self-esteem
- classmates who make fun of our imperfections
- dating relationships that lack respect and turn unhealthy and abusive

Low self-esteem leads to a destructive cycle. The more people tell us we're no good or treat us as if that were true, the more we believe it. And the more we actually think we're no good, the more we let people inside our minds and hearts.

If I have lost confidence in myself,
I have the universe against me.
RALPH WALDO EMERSON

No-Good Nikki and You

Nikki's self-condemning words demonstrated that in her heart, she honestly believed she was no good. Every botched test, every uncomfortable conversation, every embarrassing moment confirmed her conviction that she wasn't worth anything. That she didn't matter.

Because Nikki didn't really fit in, a lot of kids made fun of her, confirming the lies that echoed through her mind: *I'm no good. I'm a failure. I could never be a supergirl, so why even try?*

What about you? Does Nikki's story sound familiar? Do you hate yourself sometimes? Do you think you're just not worth it? Think about each of these questions and take the time to write down your responses.

1. Am I overly critical of myself? Do I constantly compare my body, my personality, or my gifts with what I see in other people?

2. Am I obsessed with my self-image, constantly concerned about how I look and what I say?

3. Do I fail to take care of my body and get rest because I don't think I'm worth the time?

4. Am I unsure of myself in social situations? Is finding satisfying relationships difficult for me?

5. Do I have trouble asking for what I want? Do I even *know* what I want?

6. Do I feel as if I always have to be strong for other people? Am I trying to be a supergirl?

7. Do I replay conversations in my mind, analyzing whether I said the right thing?

8. Do I respect my body, or am I okay with "whatever"?

9. Do I cut or burn my body? Pull my hair out? Starve myself?

10. Do I constantly put myself down? Do I enjoy other people's pity?

Did you learn anything about yourself? Are you living with any major insecurities? If so, don't despair! You can say goodbye to insecurity.

You don't have to go through life feeling worthless. It's okay to feel good about being you. You don't have to be tormented by thoughts that you're ugly or fat or stupid. You can be confident in the woman God's created you to be. You can learn to respect yourself and not let other people use you. You can be free!

But these things won't happen overnight. No feel-good prayer or magic pill will do the trick. Battling our insecurities requires changing the way we think and the voices we listen to.

> Praise and criticism are a lot like bubblegum.
> Chew on them for a little while, and then spit them out.
> **ANONYMOUS**

When we are living on the downside of life, an ugly pattern of comparing ourselves to others emerges. *Look at Hannah. She's the most popular cheerleader, she's always surrounded by people, and she has a hot boyfriend. Why can't I be popular? Or Josie. She's cute, and her parents can afford all the latest fashions. Why did God make me ugly? Or Katie. She's confident and smart—she gets all A's and hardly studies. Why am I so dumb?*

I wish my hair would hold curl. I wish my stomach was flatter. I try hard in school, but I still can't make A's. I don't have anybody to go to prom with. The only times the guys even notice me is when they make fun of me.

Ever felt that way? It all seems so unfair. And we wonder why God would make us inferior to the rest of the world. So day in and day out, we beat ourselves up. We mope through life feeling horrible.

I have found that as we stumble through the darkness of insignificance, we get more and more desperate for change. We frantically want somebody to tell us we're worth something. But at the end of the day, when we lie alone in the darkness of our beds, that horrible gut feeling of worthlessness is still there. Why? Because grades, boys, popularity, and success can't satisfy that emptiness and longing in our souls.

Nothing can. No guy, no GPA, and no success can totally satisfy our hearts and make us feel secure. Even Miss America struggles with self-esteem. We all do.

Remember the scene in *Ever After* when the baroness throws Danielle in the dungeon so the world will never know she's a princess? This cruel stepmother wants to keep Prince Henry's one true love locked up so he will never find her. Danielle seems destined to waste away in a dull and dreary life, spending her days scrubbing floors and cooking over a hot fire.

But fortunately for Danielle and the prince, the baroness can't stop love. And neither can the evil one stop Jesus' eternal love by trying to deceive you and me about who we are. Still, every day, Satan tries to put lies in our heads. He knows that if you and I start thinking lies—that we're worthless, no good, the scum of the earth—we'll soon accept them as truth.

God knows every single hair on your head (Matthew 10:30), every thought you think (Psalm 139:2), every tear you cry (Psalm 56:8). He knows every mole, every freckle, every imperfection. He knows your fears and feelings and pain.

But that doesn't stop His love. Nothing can.

God tells us that He delights in us (Zephaniah 3:17). He's crazy about every single girl that is living and breathing right now. That includes you! As you read these words, God is dancing and singing because He loves you. We often feel as if we're not good enough, not smart enough, not put-together enough, but God doesn't look at that stuff. God didn't create you and me for ourselves. He didn't make us for a life of existing, of drudgery, of hiding, of stabbing our own hearts with the lies of the devil.

No way. You and I were made in God's image. That means we bear the marks of God. We point people back to Him. You and I are immensely valuable for one reason—because God made us. He handcrafted us and put us together for His glory. We just need to see it and understand it.

Regardless of how we're feeling or how we've failed, the truth of who we are as God's daughters will never, ever change. Satan wants us girls to build our identity on our feelings. I don't know about you, but my feelings can change in a heartbeat. Up and down and up and down. Hey, we're girls.

Satan also wants us to define ourselves by what other people think and say. He wants us to build our identity on our accomplishments, popularity, and success. He wants us to depend on our parents' approval or our boyfriends' love.

But that kind of identity won't withstand the storms of life. When our boyfriend loses interest, when we flub up in a class presentation, when we don't get into our dream college, or when our parents say in so many words, "You'll never be good enough," we'll be devastated.

Then what? The feelings come rushing back—the I'm-no-good, I-hate-my-life, dumb-stupid-idiot feelings. Are we to sit by as victims of circumstance? Of other people? Of our own hearts?

God says *no*. When you and I choose to follow God, He begins the process of challenging the lies we believe—every single last one. God knows that each and every one of those bricks—accomplishment, popularity, success, whatever—will eventually crumble into a big pile of worthlessness.

As God's girls, we get a heart makeover! But it's not magic—no *poof!* and all your insecurities are gone. The Bible calls the process *sanctification*, and it takes our whole life long. The way we engage this process—the way we develop our self-image—is important. The Bible admonishes, "Take care to build on the foundation! Remember, there is only one foundation, the one already laid: Jesus Christ. Take particular care in picking out your building materials...If you use cheap or inferior materials, you'll be found out" (1 Corinthians 3:10-12).

As girls, our insecurities and fears can easily slip into the "building materials" of our identity. Before we know it, we're blinded to the reality of who God is and who we are as his daughters. But God's truth is powerful. Like dynamite. It can blow us girls' insecurities right up!

In order to break the chains of insecurity, we have to bring our fears to God rather than hiding from Him or pretending we're fine. We tend to feel as if we have to hide our insecurities and fears, as if pretending they're not there will make them go away. But no, it's just the opposite. God says something like this: *Give those crumbling bricks to Me. Let's get some new foundations going on. Let Me show you who you really are. Listen to My voice. Build your life with My truth. The reason you feel worthless is that you've been building your identity with no-good bricks.*

Wow. When you and I really "get" what Jesus is offering us girls, continuing to stay stuck in the hole of self-pity seems kind of stupid. What are we waiting for?

> Go out in the world and work like money doesn't matter.
> Sing as if no one is listening. Dance as if no one is watching.
> **ALAN ALDA**

Your Ticket Out

We girls can feel worthless for several destructive reasons.

- We search for our identity in people and stuff, so we hate ourselves and try to change who we are.
- We define ourselves by what we do, so when we mess up, we think we're failures.
- We listen to too many voices. We believe what other people tell us, so when somebody says we are dumb or no good, we think it must be true.

The problem is not simply that we lack confidence. We'll always lack confidence—and that's precisely the point. It's not about us. Our self-consciousness often stems from an absorption with ourselves. When we start to think life is all about us, life becomes a crazy race to get and keep people's attention.

The challenge for us as God's girls is to stop listening to the world and start listening to Jesus. To stop trying to build our own confidence and to let Him be our confidence. Face it—we're all going to fail sometimes.

God's girl doesn't settle for Satan's lies. Sure, she still struggles with insecurities. But as soon as she starts feeling no good, she runs straight to Jesus. She collects her ugly thoughts and feelings of worthlessness and puts them in Jesus' big, strong, powerful hands. God's girl cries out to Him for His help, His confidence, and reassurance of His love.

She doesn't try to go through life solo. She's real with God. And she doesn't pretend that everything is fine when her heart is being ripped apart. So how do we do it? How can we stop wallowing in our insecurities and actually fight them with truth?

Stop Believing Lies

Have you ever watched a TV show and been so caught up in it that you lost track of how many cookies you'd eaten? I have. In the same way, we girls don't always realize what we're telling ourselves.

As you go through your day today, start noticing the ways you tear yourself down with your words and thoughts. Let me tell you, examples will pop up everywhere. Successfully battling our insecurities means we have to stop telling ourselves these lies. The Bible says it like it is: "Be made new in the attitude of your minds" (Ephesians 4:23 NIV). Being made new is a process, but it starts right here and right now. It starts with telling ourselves the truth.

Dig into God's Truth About You

Once you and I start to identify what we're really thinking and feeling, we need to go to war. When did we ever start to think that we have to passively accept whatever we *feel* as reality? Um...not true. The weapons we fight with, though, aren't swords or bombs. Our weapons are statements of truth that blow up the chains of lies we believe. Here are a few:

- God loves me (John 3:16).
- I am free of all the penalties and punishments chalked up by all my misdeeds (Ephesians 1:7).
- I am holy (1 Peter 1:16).
- I am beautiful because God created me (Psalm 139:14).
- I am a temple of the Holy Spirit (1 Corinthians 3:16-17).
- I am healed because of Jesus' bruises (Isaiah 53:5).
- God has great plans for me (Jeremiah 29:11).

The Bible is chock-full of truth about who we are as God's girls. That's why we've got to read it—so we can know for ourselves who God created us to be instead of taking somebody else's word for it.

Realize What's Important in Life

What's God looking for? The perfect outfit? A 4.0 GPA? A wall covered with medals? Not quite. The Bible says that "GOD is always on the alert, constantly on the lookout for people who are totally committed to him" (2 Chronicles 16:9). To God, our worth is so much more than just skin deep. "God looks at the heart" (1 Samuel 16:7), and if we're going to live as His girls, that means that we should too.

Being totally committed to God doesn't mean giving away our heels, cute bags, and our makeup. But it does mean grounding our lives on more than just our looks or our accomplishments. I want to develop a heart that pleases God and take care of my body in a way that honors Him.

Live Free

Living free is hard. It's not always smooth sailing, especially when other people cut us down. But when God's girl hears unfounded criticism and cutting remarks, she guards her freedom by reminding herself that *they are not true*.

God's truth has the power to set us free from the shackles of our insecurities, but we've got to claim it for our own. As God's girls, you and I have to choose every single day to be who we are—His daughters—and not enslave ourselves to what other people say.

Hold your head high today as you walk down the hallway, along the sidewalk, or across the parking lot. You are precious to God! He treasures you! He delights in you!

In the Word

So where do we get our confidence? As girls who want to live free, this is a really important question. In *The Sound of Music*, Maria sings, "I have confidence…in me!" Is this the secret? Our culture tells us girls to find our inner strength. So is it just a matter of digging deeper? I don't know about you, but on some days, I can dig as deep as I want in my own heart and get nothing.

No wonder. The Bible actually says that to trust only in ourselves is stupid:

> Cursed is the strong one
> who depends on mere humans,
> who thinks he can make it on muscle alone
> and sets GOD aside as a dead weight (Jeremiah 17:5).

God evidently takes this stuff pretty seriously. This confidence issue isn't just icing on the cake; it's at the heart of following God. Jeremiah goes on to describe the life of someone who trusts himself:

> He's like a tumbleweed on the prairie,
>> out of touch with the good earth.
> He lives rootless and aimless
>> in a land where nothing grows (verse 6).

Hmm…not the kind of life I want to live. If we girls rely just on our own strength, we'll end up falling flat on our faces without enough confidence to get up again. We may start off strong, but eventually, when life gets hard, confidence in ourselves is going to run out. But notice how Jeremiah describes people who trust God:

> But blessed is the man who trusts me, GOD,
>> the woman who sticks with GOD.
> They're like trees replanted in Eden,
>> putting down roots near the rivers—
> Never a worry through the hottest of summers,
>> never dropping a leaf,
> Serene and calm through droughts,
>> bearing fresh fruit every season (verses 7-8).

"Putting down roots near rivers. Never a worry." That sounds pretty secure to me! As a follower of Jesus, I am so glad to know that I'm not in control of my own life! As God's girls, we don't have to conjure up confidence based on our accomplishments, our smarts, our wisdom.

As God's girls, we are significant, valuable, priceless…and we don't have to prove it because Jesus already did. We know that He thinks you and I are *to die for* because He did die for us. Now *that's* worth. By His death, He broke the chains of our insecurities so we could live free.

So what are we moping around for?

Smart Girls Remember...

- Every girl has highs and lows, but most of us live as victims of our insecurities.

- Making a mistake does not make you a failure or mean that you are good for nothing.

- Defining yourself by other people or by the way you feel at the moment will lead you down a slippery, dangerous slope.

- You are valuable and precious, not because of how smart or pretty or talented you are, but because you are God's daughter.
- God delights in you simply because you're you. You bring God glory by being you.
- Our confidence comes from God, not from ourselves.

God,

I need You. Desperately. I have absolutely zero confidence in myself. Living like this is difficult, and I am sad a lot. I see people every day who are prettier and smarter than me, and I always see something wrong with myself. I know You created every girl exactly the way You wanted her, but sometimes I don't understand. Set me free from living in bondage to all these lies. Show me who I am. I want to walk in freedom every day as Your girl and not to be chained to the insecurities I feel. I can't do this on my own. Thank You for helping me and loving me.

Amen.

6

Hanging with the Wrong Crowd

Right now, honey, the world just wants us to fit in.

HELEN IN *THE INCREDIBLES*

The movie *13 Going on 30* depicts a scenario every young girl has nightmares about. A thirteenth birthday party, a clique of cool girls (the Six Chicks), a wannabe, and a loyal friend who gets ditched. Not a good combo. Especially for a girl like Jenna, who wants to *be* somebody. Jenna's birthday wish is simple: "Someday, I'm gonna be one of the Six Chicks."

They're skinny, tall, blonde, popular, and cruel. Led by Lucy Wyman, they are some of the meanest and the most popular girls in school. Rude, bossy, and in your face—but not to Jenna. The Six Chicks crowd is her future, or so she thinks. But Jenna's best friend, Matt, can't help but call it like it is:

"I can't believe you invited those clones," Matt says.

"They're my friends," Jenna retorts.

"*Friends?* Six Chicks are not your friends, okay?" he argues. "You're so much more than they are. They're unoriginal."

"I don't wanna be original, Matty. I just wanna be cool."

Later that day, at home with her mom, Jenna motions to her flat chest as she rushes to put on heavy eyeliner and red-hot lipstick. "Look at me, Mom! These are *not* okay. They're fatal." After all, little girls don't stand a chance of being accepted into the Six Chicks. No, this society is for teenagers only, which means that Jenna *has* to be grown up—now.

Resisting her mom's encouragement to be herself, Jenna stuffs wads of Kleenex into her bra. "I don't wanna be 'beautiful in my own way'...I wanna look like *them*."

But copying the Six Chicks doesn't work out so well for Jenna. The party flops, and the birthday girl locks herself in her closet for a good cry. So much for that eyeliner now. (At least the Kleenex comes in handy!) Not the best induction to the teenage years, huh? Welcome to the crazy rat race of trying to fit in!

Face it. We don't realize how much we're influenced by peer pressure. Like Jenna, we want to be *in*. We want to be hot.

We want to be part of *them*, whoever *them* is. They might be in a clique or a club, they might be on a sports team, or they might simply sit at a table of popular girls at lunch. Whoever and wherever *they* are, we want in as soon as possible.

Sometimes we will go to extreme measures to fit in. We may not start stuffing the Kleenex, but to be honest, we do try to cover up our insecurities and copy the in crowd. This may sound like innocent fun, but we have to be careful because hanging out with the wrong crowd can seriously mess up our lives.

In this chapter, we're going to dig into our universal struggle as girls with peer pressure. Much of who you are is directly related to who you spend time with. As the old saying goes, "Show me your friends, and I will show you your future."

> I cannot and will not cut my conscience
> to fit this year's fashions.
> **LILLIAN HELLMAN**

Defining Peer Pressure

So what is peer pressure, and why is it such a big deal? I mean, friends are friends, right? My dictionary defines peer pressure as influence: "Social pressure by members of one's peer group to take a certain action, adopt certain values, or otherwise conform in order to be accepted."

Every girls wants to be normal and fit in, so peer pressure can be especially powerful in a girl's life. We all want to be loved and accepted, and we all want to have friends. But when our lives are ruled by peer pressure, we become like those we spend time with. In *13 Going on 30*, Matt calls this kind of girl a clone. She's a copy, a robot.

Being cool often requires something of us. We may have to ditch our old friends. We may have to make fun of the outcasts. We may have to change the way we dress, act, and talk. We may even have to take a dare on drugs, alcohol, or sex. Sure, being liked and hanging out with the in crowd can feel great. I know that. But it can cost a lot too. When we start hanging out with the wrong crowd, we often…

  care way too much about what other people think

  will do almost anything to fit in

  are rude and mean to people outside the group

  get a really messed-up idea of what a friend is

  become prideful and self-absorbed in our own little lives

  use people instead of caring about them

When we give in to peer pressure, we no longer value who we really are. We start defining who we are by external things like fashion, stuff, and popularity. We force square pegs (ourselves) into round holes (the peer group's characteristics) and constantly live in fear of not fitting in. And we don't see that often our new friends don't really care about us. It's really all a game.

> You don't get harmony when
> everybody sings the same note.
> **DOUG FLOYD**

Getting to Know Hip Hannah

Bret poked Hannah in the ribs as he walked by our table in the cafeteria. "What are you girls doing tonight? You should come to my party. It's gonna be *way* fun."

"Bret's family is gone for the weekend," his friend Joe added.

"Well…" Hannah looked at me awkwardly. "I dunno. I mean…my family is going over to Megan's for a barbecue."

"Oh yeah, *that* sounds like a lot of fun," Joe said sarcastically.

"Let's see, burgers with the parents or beer at my house." Brett cut in. "Tough decision. See you tonight."

Just then, the bell rang, and I was off to chemistry lab, but I couldn't forget the look on Hannah's face. She was torn, struggling to make up her mind. After all, Bret and Joe were two of the hottest guys in school.

I'd been invited to my share of parties, but I also tried to stay away from certain places and from certain people I knew would be a bad influence. But Hannah didn't know. She had just transferred in when her family moved to town.

I hope I get to see her tonight, I thought to myself. *I'll talk to her then*.

Hannah's parents showed up at my house around seven. "Where's Hannah?" I asked.

"She said she wasn't feeling well," her mom said with a sigh. "I worry about that girl sometimes."

I called Hannah's cell, but it went directly to voice mail.

At five the next morning, my cell woke me up. "Megan, I need your help. I…I went to Bret's house last night. You know, just to check it out. It was great. We were just hanging out and dancing, and I met a bunch of Bret's friends, and…" Hannah's voice broke off.

"We ended up in Bret's room. A bunch of his friends were in there too. And he…he started pulling my shirt off. I told him no, but he kept saying we should have sex…" She paused as she broke into sobs.

"Megan," she cried. "I don't know what to do."

Every girl struggles with peer pressure. We want to fit in, to be liked, to be surrounded by friends. After all, nobody wants to be in the *out* crowd. But for Hannah, this desire to fit in controlled her life. She seemed to be unable to say no to anyone, especially the hottest guy in school.

Have you ever met a girl like this? She's the one who hangs out with you as if you're good friends, but suddenly she's gone, talking to the hot dude who just walked in. Don't be shocked. Regardless of how many laughs you shared, how many times she told you what a great friend you were, she was lying. As soon as Hip Hannah finds a cooler friend to hang out with, you're gone. Especially if it's a guy!

Falling into this mind-set is easy for us girls. After all, we all want to be liked. We all want friends. But sometimes peer pressure can drive us to do things we said we would never do. Hanging out with the wrong crowd can make us cruel, heartless, and stupid. All we want is to be *in,* and we'll do anything to get there.

> I think I would have folded to the peer pressure if
> I didn't have my mom to encourage me to be me.
> **LISA LESLIE**

So what's the big deal about fitting in? Why does it even matter who we hang out with? Why does the desire for friends hold so much power in a girl's life?

Friendships are really important to us girls. They can seem more important than school, more important than sports, and even more important than our family. But friendships can also make us blind. In a recent survey, researchers asked teens some pretty specific questions about peer pressure. Here's what they found:

- 41 percent of the teens had teased people they actually liked just because their friends teased those same people.

- 36 percent had pressured friends into doing something they weren't comfortable with.

- 30 percent had folded to pressure to do something they knew was illegal.

- 42 percent had lied about liking something just so their friends wouldn't make fun of them.

- 28 percent had lied to their parents because their friends told them to.

GIRLS LIKE YOU AND ME HAD THIS
TO SAY ABOUT PEER PRESSURE...

"You don't have to look or dress or talk just like everybody else. Sometimes being cool is just being comfortable in your own skin."
—JENNA

"Friends and feelings ran my life as a teenager. It was one crazy, unpredictable ride. If I could do it all over again, I would forget being popular and hang out with people who really cared about me."
—HEATHER

"The influence of your friends can get you in deep trouble!"
—LILLIE

"My life is like a constant roller coaster. I try to be happy and please my friends and do things to seem cool, but then I feel guilty because I do stuff I know is wrong."
—HANNAH

"I have tons of regrets because of giving in to peer pressure, but thankfully, they are covered by the blood of Christ."
—PAM

"Friends are a big deal. Choose your friends carefully. Don't just hang out with anybody."
—NIKKI

"I used to hang out with the people who were the most popular because I cared more about what people thought about me than what was best for me."
—KAREN

Across the board, these teens agreed that peer pressure is a significant issue regardless of where a girl lives or how much money her parents make.

The survey asked, "How has peer pressure affected you?" Here are some responses:

> "I get dragged into stuff that I don't think is right."
>
> "It has made me more self-conscious."
>
> "It has made me go against what I believe in."
>
> "It has led me into bulimia and drinking."

What about you? Has trying to fit in led you to make some bad decisions? Friendships are powerful because the people who are close to us shape who we girls become. As you and I are trying to figure out this thing called life, we desperately need good, solid friends who will really care. A true friend won't push you to compromise—ever.

Hip Hannah and You

Hannah's desire to fit in and be popular led her into a shallow existence that turned destructive. She knew how to get attention. She knew how to manipulate guys. But inside, I wonder if Hannah was really as confident as she portrayed herself. Living to be popular always makes us girls insecure.

We jump into the rat race of trying to keep up with the popular girl, so we bleach our hair, bake ourselves tan, glob on the makeup, pull on the skimpy clothes, and practice the swag with our noses in the air. We think that turning heads means making friends.

Does this description sound familiar? Do you hang out with the wrong crowd? Do you just want to be popular? Take a few minutes to think about each of these questions and write down your responses.

1. Do I spend more energy trying to fit in or trying to be genuine and caring?

2. How much is my identity determined by my body? By my friends?

3. Do I act or talk a certain way so other people will like me more?

4. Do I compromise my morals and values so I will fit in to a certain group of friends?

5. Who are my friends? Do the people I hang out with build me up or tear me down as a Christian?

6. How much do my friends really care about me, and how much are they just using me?

7. Would my friends still accept me if I got sick? If I had to be in a wheelchair? If my hair fell out?

8. Are my conversations shallow and foolish, or do I talk about stuff that really matters?

9. Am I so terrified of being left out that I'm willing to drink, smoke, use drugs, and play around with sex just to fit in?

10. Who am I living for—my friends or God?

Did these questions open up any new insights about yourself? We all have room to grow. Popularity is enticing. But it's also enslaving and exhausting. At the end of the day, is that what you really want your life to be about? If we turn away from solid, constructive friendships and play the popularity game so we can join another crowd, we'll eventually lose touch with who we really are, and that's a tragedy. God didn't create you to be somebody else. He created you to be you. He created me to be me.

David understood this. He told God, "You shaped me first inside, then out; you formed me in my mother's womb. I thank you, High God—you're breathtaking! Body and soul, I am marvelously made!" (Psalm 139:13-14).

Until you and I are okay with ourselves, until we really get the fact that we are beautiful and precious to God—even with our flyaways and our moles and all the little things we wish we could change—we will always be out to try and prove our worth.

When God looks at you and me, He looks past our makeup and looks at our hearts. And right here, right now, God wants us to be free and confident in His love. You don't have to do anything to get God's attention. You just have to humble yourself and listen. God says, "Now listen, daughter, don't miss a word: forget your country, put your home behind you. Be here—the king is wild for you. Since he's your Lord, adore him" (Psalm 45:10-11).

God is wild about us? I took a little while to understand and believe that, but it's true. He loves us!

You and I were created for so much more than just fitting in. We were created to be pictures of God to the world. Think about this. If we talk and act and dress just like the world, how will they ever know the difference?

Fitting in is easy. Standing out is hard, but it's also the most freeing thing ever. When we know who we are—valuable and loved daughters of Jesus—we don't have to prove anything to anybody. Of course, that doesn't mean we shouldn't take care of ourselves, be kind, and enjoy friendships. But it does mean that our motive is different, and we don't have to compromise what we believe just to be accepted by people who don't have our best interests in mind.

We don't have to fit in! Rather than conforming to the popular crowd, God wants you and me to be secure in Him. Remember what we saw in Romans 12:2?

> Don't become so well-adjusted to your culture that you fit into it without even thinking. Instead, fix your attention on God. You'll be changed from the inside out…Unlike the culture around you, always dragging you down to its level of immaturity, God brings the best out of you, develops well-formed maturity in you.

Think about it. What do you and I want to be known for? When your friends think about you, what's the first thing they think of? Awesome hair? Hot body? The queen of fashion?

Or do they think you're kind, caring, genuine, real, and honest? Do they notice that you're comfortable in your own skin? Do people just think of your beautiful face, or do they remember your beautiful heart—a heart that loves God and cares about other people?

Any girl can fit in. That actually doesn't require much. But only God's girl can stand out and be confident in her own world. Girl, you and I don't have to give in to the pressure to fit in. We don't need alcohol or drugs to feel good, and we don't have to play around with sex to be sexy.

Our goal in life is not to be the most popular girls on campus. Instead, we should be on the lookout for a few good, legit friends who won't ignore us if we get a zit. Friends who will love us as we are and be there for us. Who will give us the freedom to be ourselves instead of pressuring us to change who we are. Friends who won't walk out when we need them most.

A real friend likes to have fun. She can laugh, cry, and live life with you. You can be real with her. She loves you not because of what you wear, but because of who you are. Friends like that are few and far between. But they're real.

> Do not follow where the path may lead. Go, instead, where there is no path and leave a trail.
> **RALPH WALDO EMERSON**

Your Ticket Out

We girls can be lured into hanging out with the wrong crowd for several reasons.

- We have a messed-up idea of what it takes to be a good friend, so our lives are all about being hip and hot, and we neglect developing loving hearts.
- We are terribly afraid of being all alone, so we're willing to do anything—even destructive things—just to fit in.
- We don't want to judge, so we accept and hang out with anybody, even those who use us.

So what's a girl to do? Maybe as you've been reading, you've realized that you're a little like Hip Hannah. Every day, all of us girls face the temptation to be like her. And if we don't know who we are as God's girls, we will all fall into the rut of hanging out with the wrong friends and making bad decisions.

Who are your friends? Do they really care about each other...about you? Finding good, solid friends can be hard sometimes. Really hard. Maybe you feel like the only girl at your whole school who doesn't want to be obsessed with boys, being sexy, and fitting in.

Do you feel alone? Talk to God about it. After all, He cares about the intimate details of His girls' lives. He's not going to ask you to follow Him and then hang you out to dry. Solid, life-changing friends—girls and guys who will stick with you no matter what—are a huge blessing from God. You can't just make deep friendships happen, but you can make sure you're headed in the right direction.

> Blessed is the man
>   who does not walk in the counsel of the wicked
> or stand in the way of sinners
>   or sit in the seat of mockers. (Psalm 1:1 NIV)

> Don't assume that you know it all.
>   Run to GOD! Run from evil! (Proverbs 3:7).

Are we girls running toward God or toward destructive friendships? Are we putting ourselves in difficult situations, going to parties and hanging out with friends who we know will lead us to compromise?

It's not worth it. Regardless of how amazing the party is, how great the rave, how high the high, or how hot the guy, when it's over, we're left feeling empty, guilty, and alone. Hanging out with the wrong crowd may seem fun at first, but it never satisfies. Never.

What does a girl like who isn't controlled by peer pressure? This kind of girl is okay with just being herself. She's not controlled by other people, and she doesn't give in to the pressure of the popular crowd. She doesn't lower herself to mess around with stuff she knows will only take her down. She doesn't bother with being stupid or extreme. She's confident, secure, and genuine. She understands God's love for her, and she doesn't degrade herself by settling for a cheap imitation. She lives for more than turning heads.

Every day, with every breath, God's girl wants to make God look big. She doesn't try to steal glory or attention for herself. And she knows that her true friends will point her toward God and never pressure her to turn away from Him.

So how can we girls break free from the shackles of peer pressure?

Know Who You Are

We girls can be duped into defining ourselves by our friends and especially by our guy. But when we do, we're like Jell-O. We have to shift and change a lot.

I don't know about you, but I want my life to stem from my inner strength and my love for God, not just my looks. Rather than being consumed with fitting in, I want to be bold. I want to stand out against cultural lies that tell us we have to show off our bodies or win beer pong or have sex with our boyfriends to feel valuable and loved. I want to help other girls get free from the lie that they have to be party girls to enjoy life.

Let's start a new trend of respecting ourselves so much that guys can't use us. A trend of caring about other people rather than making fun of the outcasts. A trend of living confidently as God's daughters rather than settling for cheap and shallow imitations of what God wants for our lives.

Take Stock of Your Friendships

Maybe you're a lot like Hip Hannah. Or maybe you're dying to be like her. God created every single girl as beautiful, but when you and I rely on our beauty, we're setting ourselves up for heartbreak and destruction. It can happen to anyone. God said it happened to His own people: "Your beauty went to your head" (Ezekiel 16:15). And the results weren't pretty.

True friends care about each other's hearts, not just their looks. If you hang out with people just to be seen around them, to look good and build your status, maybe you need to think again.

If the girls and guys we hang out with are constantly pressuring us to change for the worse and to compromise, let's be honest. It's probably time for some new friends.

Seek Out (and Pray for) Godly Friends

Do you have any close friends who really care about you? Or are you just another girl in the crowd? Are people hanging out with you because of your stuff, or do they really care about you?

Would they be there for you in the middle of the night if your world fell apart and you needed a shoulder to cry on? Do your friends have depth of character? Do they challenge you to know Jesus more? Or are they constantly trying to get you to loosen up, to compromise, to try out some new but destructive experiences?

Our friends can shape our lives or destroy them, so we need to choose carefully. This isn't a matter of judging, but face it—you will become like the people you hang out with. As God's girls, we should be friendly with everyone, but we should also be careful about whom we get really close to.

If you feel lonely right now, as if you're the only girl out there who doesn't want to mess around with sin, talk to Jesus about it every day. Ask Him to give you wisdom in friendships and to bring genuine, real, caring friends into your life.

God *is* faithful. He knows what we need before we even ask Him (Matthew 6:8). And that includes friends.

Don't Flirt with Sin

But Megan, you might be thinking, *I would never do any of that stuff. Sure, my friends do, but I wouldn't.* Well, as my dad says, never say never! The greatest Christian can fall when the conditions are right.

Even the strongest girl will give in to what she knows is wrong if she puts herself in situations where temptation runs wild. The Bible doesn't beat around the bush: "Run away from infantile indulgence. Run after mature righteousness—faith, love, peace—joining those who are in honest and serious prayer before God" (2 Timothy 2:22). "Bad company corrupts good character" (1 Corinthians 15:33 NIV).

If you and I want to pursue God, we have to surround ourselves with people "who are in honest and serious prayer before God." Perfect people? No. But girls and guys who want to know God, who want to live their lives for more than just having fun.

> It is better to be alone than in bad company.
> **GEORGE WASHINGTON**

In the Word

The Native American word for *friend* literally means "one who carries my sorrows on his back." Wow. That's very different from "somebody cool to hang out with"!

God's Word has a lot to say about friends. In fact, my Bible version mentions *friend* 172 times! Friendship is a big deal to God because He created us as relational beings. Relationships have the potential to bring us laughter and joy as well as heartbreak and tears.

What does God want for His girls? His Word show us that God's girl...

is cautious in friendship (Proverbs 12:26 NIV)

doesn't hang out with people who are deliberately disobeying God (Psalm 1:1)

seeks out friends who will sharpen her (Proverbs 27:17)

is honest with her friends even when the truth hurts (Proverbs 27:6)

The decisions you and I make about our friends will help determine who we become five, ten, fifteen years down the road. The Bible says, "Become wise by walking with the wise; hang out with fools and watch your life fall to pieces" (Proverbs 13:20).

None of us girls want our lives to fall to pieces, but a lot of us are so hungry for acceptance, we hang out with foolish, immature friends who pull us down into sin. If we want to live as God's girls, *that* has got to change.

No, it won't be easy. Yes, people will make fun of us. But honestly, who cares? When I'm tempted to feel left out and uncool, I try to remember that knowing Jesus should radically change the way we girls live: "Our old way of life was nailed to the Cross with Christ, a decisive end to that sin-miserable life—no longer at sin's every beck and call...Sin speaks a dead language that means nothing to you; God speaks your mother tongue, and you hang on every word. You are dead to sin and alive to God" (Romans 6:6,11).

To live as God's girls, we're going to have to tell some people goodbye. Not because they're horrible and evil, but because hanging out with them will hinder us from really running after God.

If we girls want to really get serious about following God, living for Him, and knowing Him rather than doing things that turn us away from Him and then playing the Christian game on Sunday, we're going to have to take a stand for truth, purity, righteousness, and obedience. Yes, I know this is the road less traveled. But it's the best way—the only way—to really be free.

> If fifty million people do a foolish thing, it is still a foolish thing.
> **ANATOLE FRANCE**

Smart Girls Remember...

- All of us want to fit in. But in a sinful world, God's girl stands out.

- Hanging out with the wrong friends will lead even the strongest girl to compromise.

- Just because something's *cool* doesn't mean it's right. Or godly.

- Choose your friends not just because they're hot or hip, but because they love God.

- If you hang out with the crowd, you'll be mediocre. If you really pursue Jesus, your life will look different.

Jesus,

I need help. I've been hanging out with some friends who are dragging me down. I want to follow You, God, but it's hard. I don't think I have the strength to do it on my own because I tend to just follow the crowd. I want to run after You, God. I don't want to merely say that; I want to actually do it. Help me to see that being cool isn't what life is all about. God, I really need godly friends. Please bring guys and girls into my life who want to know You and live holy, God-honoring lives.

Amen.

7

Drifting Through Life

Wherever you are, be all there. Live to the hilt
every situation you believe to be the will of God.

JIM ELLIOT

lice in Wonderland was one of my favorite bedtime stories as a little girl. Following the White Rabbit down his burrow, I easily lost myself in a world where animals talk, where playing cards have tea, and where the Cheshire Cat perched in a tree offers Alice unexpected advice about life.

> "Would you tell me, please, which way I ought to go from here?"
>
> "That depends a good deal on where you want to get to," said the Cat.
>
> "I don't much care where—" said Alice.
>
> "Then it doesn't matter which way you go," said the Cat.
>
> "—so long as I get *somewhere*," Alice added as an explanation.
>
> "Oh, you're sure to do that," said the Cat, "if you only walk long enough."

Poor, lost Alice. What started out as a lazy sunny afternoon by the river's bank spiraled into a world gone mad. And Alice had no idea where she was or where she was going.

Ever felt that way? I have.

Sure, you and I don't live in Wonderland, but our world can be equally confusing. As young women, we're faced with a ton of decisions. *What to do this summer? Where to go to college? Whom to date? What to do with my life?*

And on and on and on it goes. Just like Alice, we have big questions. Just like Alice, we often don't even know what we want. We have no Cheshire Cat to point us in the right direction, just a great big future with a million and one possibilities and a million and one ways we can mess up our lives.

Or so we think. Looking at the big, scary future, all we see is one big question mark. One of the scariest parts about growing up is realizing that our decisions actually have a big impact on where we end up and whom we end up with. Sometimes I just wish I could be a little girl again and let Mom and Dad figure it out!

As I sorted through college application packets, career test results, and job applications, drifting sure sounded like a good option. Forget the stress, the headache, and the endless decisions.

And just *be.* Sleep till noon. Watch *The Bachelor* and *Gilmore Girls.* Hang out with friends. Shop until I drop. Take a nap. Grab some dinner. Catch a movie. Surf Facebook. Jam to late-night music. And fall into bed exhausted to do it all over again and again and again.

Sound like the dream life? Maybe that's kind of extreme, but don't you wish sometimes that life was one big vacation? No responsibility, no worries, just living it up?

The "totally chill" life may sound like fun, but you and I were created for more than just existing. In this chapter, we're going to consider what a life without purpose looks like. In contrast, we'll see how much God has planned for us as His daughters. We'll discover what our passions are and start dreaming God-sized dreams for our lives rather than being paralyzed by our fears and insecurities.

Defining *Lost*

So what do we mean by "drifting through life"? Drifting is a mind-set and a lifestyle of not using time, opportunities, or energy to any good purpose. The lost girl lacks self-confidence and is crippled by her fear of failing, of missing God's will.

When we work up the courage to pull our heads out of the sand, we see that we can't hide from the big life choices we need to make. And yes, they can be intimidating. Welcome to the club! We're all unsure about the future, especially as young women. But we begin to drift when we stop picturing where we'd like to get and just start to exist. One of the biggest mistakes we can make is to stop asking God what we should do and start trying to figure it all out on our own. As girls, we drift through life when we…

> stop seeking God's heart
>
> are paralyzed by fear of failure
>
> lose faith in God's desire to work through us
>
> give up on pursuing our passions
>
> forget who we are and whose we are
>
> focus only on being happy and having fun

Ever notice how easily little kids can dream crazy big dreams? One day they will climb Mount Everest, find a cure for cancer, or travel to the moon. Why is that? Kids don't say, "I can't." They say, "Why not?"

Somewhere along the way from the world of Barbie and Ken to young adult life, we girls stop dreaming. Somehow we forget how big our God really is. We forget that with a single word, He beamed this world into existence. We forget that He holds together every star, every grain of sand, every hair on our heads, and every one of the 10 trillion cells in our bodies.

Without a firm conviction that God has big dreams for our lives, we start to wander from one thing to the next without any purpose for our actions. We're continually torn by opportunities in our lives, unable to decide on what to do.

Instead of pursuing God's dreams for us, we label our once passionate hearts as young, immature, and unrealistic, and we sink into a life of empty mindless amusements. We become convinced that drifting is normal and think that life is all about having fun. Settling in with a big coke and a tub of popcorn, we watch the movie of life without even considering what our role is.

> We are limited, not by our abilities, but by our vision. The most pathetic person in the world is someone who has sight, but no vision.
> **HELLEN KELLER**

Getting to Know Lost Laura

Sitting across from me at Starbucks as we sipped our carmel macchia-tos, Laura filled me in on her life at college.

In high school, Laura volunteered at the community center down-town tutoring kids. Back then, she talked nonstop about someday moving to New York and teaching in the inner city. After high school graduation, she headed to a prestigious state university that was known for its educa-tion program. But now, after her first semester of college, I didn't sense the same passion in my dear friend's voice.

"I'm just not really sure anymore," Laura said with a shrug of her shoul-ders. "I dunno. I used to think I was supposed to be a teacher, but now I just don't know if I could handle it. *Every day?* Besides, the classes are so hard. I never get to have any fun. It's just work, work, work."

"So what are you going to do?" I asked her.

"I think I'm dropping out of school," Laura said with a sigh. "I'm failing half my classes anyway, and honestly, I just don't care anymore. I think I'll just move back home and relax for a while. College is so stressful."

"But what about teaching?"

"Oh, maybe later. Not right now. I mean, Megan, we're only young once. I want to take some time off to have some fun. Hey…" Laura leaned across the table with a glimmer in her eyes. "You and me and Hailey…we could move to New York and just *enjoy* life for a while. Huh? Wouldn't that be a blast!"

In Laura's mind, life was all about having fun. I get that, but my bril-liant and talented high school friend was throwing away her lifelong dream of teaching on a whim simply because things got hard. We girls tend to think that the easy way is the best way, but living God's dream is about way more than just partying it up.

Sure, we all need downtime. But too often, you and I are tempted to set aside the passions God has given us, to stop running after God's heart, and to just chill. But if you add up a whole life of just having fun, just chillin', you'll see a life that is *wasted.*

As God's girls, we need wisdom and courage to live God's dream for us—even when it is hard or scary. Otherwise, you and I will just exist.

Why is it so hard sometimes to make decisions and figure out what God wants for us?

GIRLS LIKE YOU AND ME HAD THIS
TO SAY ABOUT MAKING BIG DECISIONS...

"Sometimes I'm scared to death of missing God's will for my
life. But when we actually 'get' that God is guiding our every
step, it's the most freeing thing ever. If you are seeking God—
not just His will, but God Himself—you can't mess up your life."
—JESSICA

"I struggle with self-worth, and I'm always comparing myself
with other girls. In the past, I constantly lived in fear of failing, but
I'm becoming more confident in who God made me to be."
—ANNE

"God put us together exactly the way He wanted to. I wish I had
realized this before and worked hard to improve my giftings
instead of being jealous of girls who had talents that I didn't have."
—LYDIA

"I used to be so caught up in fear of doing the wrong thing or
making God mad. I was one scared, miserable girl, running around
like crazy trying to make sure that God loved me. I really, really
wish someone had shared with me what grace means: that God
loves you and me as we are, not some future better version."
—EMILY

"If you feel paralyzed about the future, don't look at
the horizon. What has God laid out directly in front
of you? What's your next step? That's God's will."
—KATHRYN

"The only way to make solid, godly decisions is to get
close to God. Ditch the checklist of dos and don'ts
and dive headfirst into knowing Jesus for yourself."
—JULIE

Sure, we may pretend we've got it all together, but inside, we're often insecure. We're so worried or scared that we get freaked out and start doubting God or questioning our sanity. But we hide it all behind a pasted-on smile.

A recent study found that even though we may appear to have it all together, many of us are confused and worried about our futures. Only one in five young people say they have "found something meaningful to dedicate their lives to." Twenty-five percent of young people are disengaged with life and aren't actively pursuing their dreams.[1]

Being young women isn't just about figuring out what in the world we want to do with our lives. It's more about figuring out who we are. In the process of developing our own unique identity, we often...

don't pursue our talents for fear of failure

worry about making wrong choices and messing up our lives

feel as if we're living for someone else

change our majors, our jobs, or our relationships for fear of commitment[2]

The stress we put on ourselves takes its toll on our bodies, our moods, and our emotions. Research indicates that lack of purpose in a girl's life is directly linked with depression, substance abuse, low self-esteem, and suicide.

Tragically, many of us want to fit in so badly that we quit dreaming God's dreams. We give up on developing our talents. We drop out of school. We let our friendships die. We just drift, and life doesn't seem worth living anymore.

It hurts to want everything and nothing at the same time.
MICHELLE BRANCH

Lost Laura and You

"I'm just not really sure anymore...I think I'll just move back home and relax for a while." Laura's dilemma about school and life revealed her fear of failure, which crippled her from pursuing God's dreams for her life.

What about you? Can you identify with Laura? Are you just drifting through life? Maybe reflecting on these questions and writing down your answers will help you find out.

1. What are my dreams? What goals will help me experience my dreams?

2. Am I passionate about anything, or am I just existing?

3. Do I merely tolerate life and live for the weekends?

4. Do I spend all my free time chillin' with friends, watching TV, and surfing the Internet?

5. Do I just go with the flow, or am I intentional about the decisions I make?

6. Am I often depressed because my life is so small and insignificant?

7. What am I good at? Am I diligently developing my natural talents so God can work through me?

8. When was the last time I dreamed and prayed about what God wants to accomplish through me?

9. What motivates my life right now—having fun? Getting other people to like me? Accomplishing a lot? Pleasing God?

10. What would I do if I knew I couldn't fail and money was not an issue?

Did you learn anything about yourself as you considered these questions? If you're discovering that you're a drifter, don't despair! The good news is that Lost Laura and you and I are not doomed to lives of disillusionment and failure.

You can discover what you're naturally good at and begin developing your gifts and talents right now. You can stop just existing and begin to confidently pursue God's dream for your life. You can discover a purpose for your life that is way more fulfilling than living from one party, one weekend, or one thrill to the next.

Have you ever had a "life freak-out" moment? You're doing home-work, watching TV, brushing your teeth, whatever...and *bam*—out of nowhere the thought hits: *What am I doing with my life? It's flying by, and I don't have a clue.*

Sometimes just thinking about the future overwhelms me. Boy, it would sure be nice if our life plan came nicely shrink-wrapped with in-structions delivered by God-mail the moment we accepted Christ!

As I talk to girls all across the country, I keep running into the same question: "Megan, how do I discover God's will for my life? How do I know what to do next?"

As young women, we can easily obsess about the future. We can also let fear and uncertainty cripple us from actually taking a step. Some girls talk about finding God's will as if it's a treasure hunt gone bad. *What if I miss God's will? What if I make the wrong choice? What if I mess up my entire life because I do X rather than Y?*

Is God deviously hiding His plan and His blessings from us just to make life hard?

Wait a minute! This is *not* the God you and I follow and serve. Once and for all, let's clear up the confusion about God's will. Nowhere in the Bible does God ever say to look for His will in a certain major or a cer-tain career.

We tend to think of God's will as a program—a one-time download from God's heart to the hard drive of our brains. So we worry ourselves to death in fear that we'll blink, miss the memo, and be doomed for life. What a small view of God!

His will for your life is so much bigger than a specific major or a cer-tain career. His will for your life is to become more like Him. Look at what the New Testament says about God's will for you and me:

- "It is God's will that you should be sanctified" (1 Thessalo-nians 4:3 NIV).

- "Now we ask you, brothers, to respect those who work hard among you, who are over you in the Lord and who admon-ish you. Hold them in the highest regard in love because of their work. Live in peace with each other. And we urge you, brothers, warn those who are idle, encourage the timid, help the weak, be patient with everyone. Make sure that nobody

pays back wrong for wrong, but always try to be kind to each
other and to everyone else. Be joyful always; pray continually;
give thanks in all circumstances, for this is God's will for you
in Christ Jesus" (1 Thessalonians 5:12-18 NIV).

God wants us to be sanctified, which means to be holy and pure. He
desires for us to love and honor others, to live at peace with others, to be
joyful, to live with a grateful heart, and to pray continually so we never
forget the blessing we have of knowing God personally even when life
gets hard.

God's Word has a whole lot more to say about obedience than about
a one-time download of God's will. A mentor of mine recently helped me
clear up the confusion with this

God's will = obedience

Discovering God's will is not a one-time event. It involves a day-in, day-
out lifestyle of obeying what we know and trusting God with what we
don't yet know.

I get it, Megan, you might be saying. *But what does obedience look like?
How can I know if I'm in God's will?* Look again at Romans 12:1-2:

Take your everyday, ordinary life—your sleeping, eating, going-
to-work, and walking-around life—and place it before God
as an offering. Embracing what God does for you is the best
thing you can do for him...God brings the best out of you,
develops well-formed maturity in you.

God's dream for our lives is way bigger than just a well-paying career,
job security, a great marriage, and a long, relaxed retirement. Every second, every breath is a gift from our Creator, and we were created to bring
Him glory. That's the reason you and I exist—to bring God glory. To point
back to Him. Reality check—this life is *not* ultimately about us or about
getting what we want. We were created for God.

Whatever we are doing—eating or drinking or studying or working
or playing or hanging out with friends—we should do it not for our own
glory, but to point back to Jesus.

"Whatever you do, do it all for the glory of God" (1 Corinthians 10:31

NIV). That's pretty all-inclusive. Apparently, in the death of our normally self-absorbed lives, even the ordinary things can gain meaning. When we abandon normal life, things finally start to make sense because suddenly, all of it—every single last thing we do—gains a purpose greater than just the task itself.

Our world puts the spotlight on success and accomplishment, but Jesus seems to be asking us, "What good does it do you to get everything you want? To be rich and famous? To be popular? To gain the whole world? What good is any of it if you lose your soul? If you don't know Me?" (paraphrase of Matthew 16:26).

In this verse, Jesus gets to the heart of our life's purpose. We girls can lose ourselves and start to drift through life like Lost Laura when we pursue small dreams, like money, success, and popularity. And we forget that all this stuff is temporary. As young women trying to make practical decisions, we get distracted so quickly. And we forget that we have something bigger to live for!

You and I drift through life when we live to...

> make other people happy
>
> accomplish things and build our own little kingdoms
>
> experience pleasure, cramming in the most fun possible
>
> find acceptance, security, and delight in anything besides Jesus Christ

God's girls have only one unchanging purpose for life, one aim to run after that will always satisfy. One of my favorite authors, John Piper, writes, "If my life was to have a single, all satisfying, unifying passion, it would have to be God's passion."[3]

Let's face it. Anything else is just not big enough.

> You see things and say, "Why?"
> but I dream things and say, "Why not?"
> **GEORGE BERNARD SHAW**

Your Ticket Out

We girls can feel lost for several reasons:

- We don't know who we are. Every decision becomes an identity crisis, so we make our decisions to make other people (or a guy) happy.

- We are paralyzed by insecurities and are deathly afraid of failing, so we don't pursue the talents God has given us. We just exist.

- We think that life is all about money, popularity, and success, so when this stuff doesn't satisfy our souls, we become disillusioned drifters.

What's a girl to do? Maybe as you've been reading, you've realized that you can identify with Lost Laura. We all can to some degree because we all occasionally feel overwhelmed thinking about the uncertainties of the future. The problem comes when our fear roots our feet in one spot and we exchange our God-sized dreams for puny replicas. Setting aside our God-given passions for a life of fun and ease may sound great—as it did to Laura—but the stakes are way higher than we think.

As God's girls, each of us has a unique and specific role to play in the telling of God's story. If you and I wait until every single obstacle is worked out, we'll never accomplish anything. Planning is an important part of the journey, but we have to let God direct our steps. "We plan the way we want to live, but only GOD makes us able to live it" (Proverbs 16:9).

What does a girl look like who is pursuing God's passions for her life? The girl with a clear focus knows who she is and whom she's following. She is humble and yet unashamed about pursuing the passions God has laid on her heart. She's free to become the woman God has created her to be instead of settling for the easy way out just to avoid the possibility of failure. She's confident that she's not going through life alone, as God promises in Psalm 32:8 (ESV): "I will instruct you and teach you in the way you should go; I will counsel you with my eye upon you."

This young woman tries to focus on obeying God right now, not just daydreaming about the future. She realizes that life is precious, and every day she tries to make a difference in someone else's life instead of focusing only on her own fun little kingdom.

So how can we stop merely existing and begin to dream God-sized dreams for our lives?

Do What You Love to Do

Sometimes we girls tend to over-spiritualize the obvious. When God made you, He handcrafted everything about you, including your talents and your personality. Jesus tells the story of a king who entrusted each of his servants with specific talents: "To one he gave five talents of money, to another two talents, and to another one talent, each according to his ability" (Matthew 25:15 NIV). You and I are a lot like these servants. God has wired each of us with particular things that we're good at. Things that we love to do. Things that make us feel alive. As you're grappling with big decisions about school, relationships, and direction in life, consider how your passions fit in to a job field or ministry. If you're unsure what you actually *love* to do, look at how you spend your free time.

Another great way to figure out what to do is to ask your family and your friends what they believe you're good at. Your friends often know you better than anybody else does. My dad always encouraged me to ask myself, if I could do anything I wanted and money wasn't an issue, what would I do?

What are you most passionate about? What do you love to do? Do it.

Dream a God-Sized Dream

I'll never forget the day Heather Mercer spoke at a chapel service at our school! A survivor of three months in captivity by the Taliban, Heather was literally bubbling over with passion for people to know Jesus' name and glory.

"What would your life look like if you had nothing to lose? What would your life look like if you had nothing to prove?" Heather asked us. "That's the call of God on your life.

"As we pursue the dreams of God, a choir of voices often emerges and says things like, 'Are you crazy? Have you lost your mind?' But God is looking for people who will say, 'I will waste my life on the purposes of Your heart.'"[4]

Are you willing to devote your life to a dream so big that other people may look at you and think you're crazy? As I walked away from that chapel, my heart couldn't help but beat a little faster. God wants you and me to dream big! Our God is powerful. He is mighty to save, and He chooses to reveal His love and heart to the world through us.

Why do we dream small? Why do we just exist? Why do we mope around? "God can do anything, you know—far more than you could ever imagine or guess or request in your wildest dreams! He does it not by pushing us around but by working within us, his Spirit deeply and gently within us" (Ephesians 3:20).

James Collins and Jerry Porras introduced the term BHAG (Big Hairy Audacious Goal—pronounced BEE-hag) in their 1996 article "Building Your Company's Vision." Begin working today toward developing a BHAG for your own life—a vision to make your life count for God.

Expose the Enemy's Lies

To paralyze us girls and keep us from obeying God, Satan tries to fill our minds with lies like these:

> I'm no good.
>
> I can't do this.
>
> My life is a failure.
>
> God has forgotten me.

Every single one of these statements is 100 percent false. Nonetheless, lies like these often cripple you and me and keep us from running after God. Many times, we stumble through life with no plan or goal for the future. We're lonely, empty, and afraid of failing.

Even when we feel small and insignificant, we can be confident as God's girls that God has brought us to the kingdom "for just such a time as this" (Esther 4:14).

Challenge Your View of God's Will

As girls, it's easy to make decisions based on how we feel. This works fine when we're picking ice cream flavors, but in real life, our decisions carry much more weight. Rather than depending on our emotions, we can look to the Bible for help as we develop a solid understanding of God's calling on our lives. We need to know we're making biblical decisions and not just riding the roller coaster of emotions.

Take some time to look up these verses and see how these statements apply not only to Abraham but also to you:

- The calling of God does not depend on your own perception of your abilities. Abraham was 75 years old when God asked him to leave his home (Genesis 12:1,4).

- God will call you to do something bigger than you could do on your own. God promised Abraham that he would be the father of many nations, but at the time, he was living as a nomad (Genesis 17:4-8).

- When we understand what God is calling us to do, our proper response is to humble ourselves. Abraham fell face-down (Genesis 17:3).

- God always calls us away from sin. He called Lot and his family out of the wickedness of Sodom and commanded them not to look back, let alone go back (Genesis 19:12-17).

- God calls us to Himself. Details may change with time, but the objective remains the same. God took Joseph into Egypt but called the Israelites out of Egypt. Both events served a purpose in God's plan to make Israel a great nation and to glorify Himself.

- The calling of God is simply to obey and trust that even when we're confused, God knows exactly what He's doing. Abraham's story is about one man learning to obey God. Despite his screw-ups, God worked in and through him.

In the Word

As Jesus' daughters, we don't need to get stressed about specific aspects of the future—where or when or who or how. We just need to *obey.* The best anecdote to freak-outs is undoubtedly bird watching! "Look at the birds, free and unfettered, not tied down to a job description, careless in the care of God. And you count far more to him than birds" (Matthew 6:26). Are you living a free, unfettered life? Or are you tied down by worry and fear?

"What I'm trying to do here is to get you to relax...Steep your life in

God-reality, God-initiative, God-provisions. Don't worry about missing out. You'll find all your everyday human concerns will be met" (verses 31,33). Relax. Get close to God and don't worry about missing out. Does it sound too easy? Too simple? Obedience can be wicked hard sometimes, but there's no mystery about it.

Want to know God's will for your life right now? "Give your entire attention to what God is doing right now, and don't get worked up about what may or may not happen tomorrow. God will help you deal with whatever hard things come up when the time comes" (verse 34).

You and I can't control the future anyway, so why do we worry about it so much? The apostle Peter tells us, "Cast all your anxiety on him because he cares for you" (1 Peter 5:7 NIV). God's girl chooses to trust God. Rather than freaking out about what's up next, we can be confident that God is working for His glory and our good.

Smart Girls Remember...

- We can experience God's will—not through an abstract, mystical pursuit but by developing a lifestyle of obeying and trusting God.

- Don't settle for a small life. Dream so big that if God isn't in your dream, you will most certainly fail.

- If you obsess about the future, you will miss out on what God has for you today. Trust God with tomorrow, but live in the now.

- As God's daughter, you are completely free. You have nothing to lose and nothing to prove.

- Drifting through life may seem fun, but nothing short of giving God glory will satisfy the deepest longings of your soul.

Lord Jesus,

I'm feeling kind of lost right now. I've been afraid to obey You because I don't want to fail. I feel insecure, God. I don't want to

*fall on my face and be left out in the dark. Forgive me, Lord, for
pursuing my own kingdom, my own plans and dreams, without
focusing on Your heart and Your priorities for my life. I want
my life to count, God. Help me to break free from a comfortable,
easy, fun life and pursue Your vision for me. Teach me to trust
You and obey You, Jesus, even when I don't understand.*

Amen.

8

Living Without Boundaries

*Being out of control is one of the worst feelings in
the world, sometimes even worse than pain.*

TERRI GUILLEMETS

Who knew that *27 Dresses* was a picture of our lives?

Jane is the friend every girl dreams to have as her maid of honor. She takes care of a million details—the dress, the cake, the flower girl, the rings, the groom's corsage...After all, Jane has been in a few weddings before. Twenty-seven, to be exact.

From the breakfast burrito she puts on her boss's desk every morning to the insanity of being in two weddings in one evening, Jane's entire life is about making other people happy. Just one little problem. Jane is great at taking care of everybody else, but she never stops to take care of herself, and it's killing her.

"I'm not just gonna be her maid of honor. I'm gonna take care of *everything*," Jane moans to her friend Kevin.

"Why don't you just say no?" Kevin suggests. "You have said no to people before, right?"

"In this situation? Never. Not once...I can't. She's my sister."

No. One simple word. But Jane can't say it. So Kevin sets out to help her learn how.

"All right. You know what we're gonna do? We're gonna practice saying no...All right, Jane, give me 50 bucks."

"No."

"Jane, it's 50 bucks. I'll pay you back."

"No."

"Jane, I *need* you to give me 50 bucks."

"No?"

"Eh, not bad. Can I have your drink?"

"Sure."

Jane can say the word *no*, but the second she stops thinking about it, she can't help but say yes to anybody about anything. Her life is one crazy string of yeses.

On the outside, Jane seems like a sweet, kind, and put-together girl. But inside, she's unhappy and falling apart. Jane may be able to pull together a solution for a ripped wedding dress or a drooping candle, but she can't save the world (though she may die trying). People pleasing can be intoxicating, and it will get you a lot of affirmation, but it's also exhausting and empty.

A lot of us girls have a hard time saying no. Maybe our friend asks for the notes because she slept through class again. Maybe our boyfriend says, "C'mon, if you really love me, let's just do it."

No is a pretty powerful word in a girl's life. Just two little letters, but not always easy to say. If you and I can't tell other people no, we'll end up compromising, spreading ourselves too thin, and burning out. Say yes to too many things, and before you know it, life is insane. Out of control.

In this chapter, we're going to investigate what life is like when we can't say no, and we'll discover how God's girls can develop healthy boundaries that will protect our hearts and help us to live free instead of being enslaved to other people's needs.

Defining Boundaries

So what is a boundary? Are we talking picket fences and guardrails? Not quite, but you get the idea. A boundary divides one entity from another.

Without fences, my neighborhood would be overrun by dogs. Without guardrails, driving through the Blue Ridge Mountains, where I live, would be really dangerous. And without physical, emotional, and time-related boundaries, you and I will live stressed-out, frazzled, and unhealthy lives. Henry Cloud and John Townsend describe this idea really well in their book *Boundaries:*

> Boundaries define *what is me* and *what is not me.* A boundary
> shows me where I end and someone else begins, leading me
> to a sense of ownership. Knowing what I am to own and take
> responsibility for gives me freedom.[1]

Just as a fence protects what's inside and what's outside, when you and I set healthy boundaries, we protect ourselves as well as the people around us.

This can be hard for us Christians to understand. God made us to serve one another, to be there for one another. And at the core of who we are, we want to be known and loved for who we are. When this need is unmet and grows out of proportion, it can drive us to break down the healthy fences around our hearts. When that happens, anybody can walk right in and take a seat on our front porch.

After all, no girl wants to be alone. Being needed can be draining, but it gives value to our lives. It gives us something to crawl out of bed for in the morning.

So what do we do? We say yes again and again and again. Yes to driving our friend to work even when we don't have money for gas. Yes to hanging out with every single person who asks us to. Yes to helping our friend study even when we're exhausted. Yes to helping our friend move when we really need to write a paper. Yes to sharing our pens, our food, our clothes, and our makeup with any girl at school. Yes to organizing a class trip. Yes to putting together the props for the school play. Yes to…you name it. Whatever someone asks, even if it's ridiculous or wrong, we say yes. But feeling the pressure to constantly rescue our friends is kind of like bondage.

Sure, we all want to help people out. After all, being a servant is a key part of following Jesus, isn't it?

Well, yes, but when you and I feel as if we have to do everything for everybody, we're setting ourselves up for disaster. As hard as we try, no girl can do everything. We're not God, and we have only so many hours in a day. A life without boundaries is insane. The yes monster is always lurking, and when we do say no, we feel horribly guilty. So we try to just tough it up and push through, sleep less, drink more coffee, and be all things to all people.

That is, until we start feeling used, get mean and nasty, and eventually crash and burn.

When we can't tell other people no, we often…

> have overly tender hearts
>
> feel obligated to be at our friends' beck and call
>
> ditch our plans if somebody asks us for help

feel as if we're horrible when we can't rescue others

define ourselves by the way we serve other people

take on too much and feel like failures when we can't do it all

neglect our own needs—even for food and sleep

live unpredictable, erratic, and emotional lives

Worst of all, when we can't say no, we lose the joy of giving and serving. Helping other people out becomes a desperate race to feel better about ourselves, to prove something. *No* is practically a cussword for us. We're terrified of saying no because saying it sounds selfish.

> It's impossible to have a healthy friendship
> with someone who has no boundaries.
> **ROBERT BURNEY**

Getting to Know Spastic Sam

Sam is one of the sweetest, most hardworking girls I know. But her life is out of control. Sam is a double major, an honors student, and the student body vice president. She plays intramural volleyball, works a part-time job, volunteers at the YWCA, and helps lead her church youth group.

I admire Sam so much. She doesn't just drift through life—she runs! There isn't a lazy bone in that girl's body, and sometimes I wonder if she ever sleeps. Just about every time I see her, Sam is running. Literally—to class, to a meeting, or to work. This girl's legit.

The other day, I saw Sam at lunch, which is a big surprise because she usually just grabs something to go.

"Ah, Sam! I'm so glad I caught you," I said as I plopped down across the table from her with my turkey sandwich in hand. "How are you doing, girl? Like, for real. You seem so busy all the time."

"I'm good," Sam responded, "Yeah, life is busy...crazy actually. Sometimes I don't know how I'm gonna make it through the day. But you know," she continued with a smile, "God will never put more on us than we can bear, right?"

I was confused. On a certain level, what Sam said was true. But I had to ask myself whether God really wants us to run ourselves down and burn ourselves out in the name of serving Him.

"Why do you do it all, Sam?" I asked. "Why don't you ever slow down?"

"Well, people ask, and I can't turn down a good opportunity. It's weird, Megan...almost like I can't say no to anybody. I mean, just this week, with finals and everything, a lot of my friends have asked me about hitching rides. Jamie needs a ride to the airport at ten tonight, and Sarah has to be at the train station at like five tomorrow morning. Amy's bus leaves, let's see...right after lunch."

Sam spouted off the list with almost an air of pride.

"Wow. That's crazy. Did you offer to do all that?" I asked Sam. "I mean, sure, it's great that you're helping them out, but...well, you should get some rest. You have finals tomorrow, right?"

"Yeah—bio and chem," Sam groaned. "I need to study...But I'll be fine. I mean, coffee always does the trick. I had to say yes, Megan. They don't have any other way of getting home. I mean, that's what friends do, right?"

> When you respect your own no, others will too.

Ever felt like Sam? I know I have. Sometimes I feel as if my own life is out of control. Too fast, too busy, too much going on. But if you and I don't learn to tell other people no, we'll kill ourselves racing from the study group to the concert to the pickup basketball game to movie night to the coffee date to the Bible study.

That is one crazy life.

GIRLS LIKE YOU AND ME HAD THIS TO SAY ABOUT BOUNDARIES...

"Learning to tell other people no—especially people I care about—is one of the hardest things for me."
—ANNE

"I didn't set any boundaries when I was younger, and now I wish I had. I did things I regret simply because I didn't respect myself enough to say no."
—MARIE

"Sometimes, saying no isn't being selfish. It's being godly."
—CARRIE

"Don't spill your guts to everyone. Part of setting healthy boundaries is learning to protect your heart."
—JOSIE

"I always thought that boundaries were just for dating, but they're not. My life was miserably out of control until I realized that I don't have to do everything."
—AMANDA

"Sometimes I just need 'me' time. It may sound selfish, but unless I take care of myself, how can I help anybody else?"
—KATHRYN

"'Guard your heart' isn't just a Bible verse. It's real, especially for girls. If we don't, we'll end up getting our hearts broken."
—LAUREN

In order to live healthy, balanced lives, we girls have to take care of ourselves. Without boundaries—without including the word *no* in our vocabulary—we'll likely end up burning out. We'll shut down, or we'll do a mediocre job because we're trying to do too many things. Too many *good* things.

To a certain extent, every girl has a phobia about saying no. But healthy boundaries actually protect our hearts. God's girl doesn't let other people push her around.

So what's the big deal about boundaries? Why do we as girls have such a hard time saying no? Well, we live in a culture that emphasizes the freedom of the individual, so *boundaries* isn't a popular word. After all, the idea of setting limits for our lives sounds kind of restraining, confining, and even old-fashioned. Walmart even sells a line of clothing for teenagers and college students called NOBO—the abbreviation for No Boundaries.

Search their website, and you just might find some pretty sweet deals. A hot pink juniors scoop tank for $4.50. A cute floral print baby-doll dress for $14.88. A pair of stonewashed grey skinny jeans for $15.98. But No Boundaries isn't just an apparel line; it's the mind-set of a lot of girls today.

As one newspaper recently pointed out, we girls think that "it's not nice to say no, unless it's in the context of a sexual request."[2] And even then, boyfriends can be pretty persuasive. In fact, studies show that half the teens who date have gone against what they believe to please their partner.

Yes seems like such an innocent little word, but taken to the extreme, every yes tears down a little bit more of who we are. When you and I always say yes to people, even if it puts us out, we can experience some pretty unpleasant consequences:

stress	insomnia
anger	exhaustion
frustration	illness
passive-aggressive behavior	burnout

Sure, we may try to keep it all nicely bottled up, hidden behind our smile. We may tell our friends, "Hey, not a problem at all…I'd love to… Sure, anything for you." But inside, we're stretching ourselves further and further and further every time we say yes. And a girl can only stretch so far.

Spastic Sam and You

I have to do everything. That's what Sam thought. Talk about overcommitment! She habitually said yes because she believed that saying no to anybody was wrong. She didn't want to be selfish, so she continued to put herself out there. Yes, yes, yes, yes.

What about you? Does Sam's story sound familiar? Does *yes* roll off your tongue like nothing? Are you stressed out and overcommitted? Think about these questions, and take a few minutes to write out your responses.

1. Do I have a hard time saying no even when I'm frustrated and overwhelmed?

2. Do I feel guilty or controlled by other people?

3. Do I have a hard time saying how I really feel?

4. Am I afraid of hurting other people's feelings?

5. Do I fear abandonment or separateness?

6. Am I afraid that if I say no, my friends (and my boyfriend) will reject me?

7. Do I manipulate people into doing things I want them to?

8. Can I take responsibility for my own life?

9. Do I feel the compulsive need to help other people all the time?

10. Are my attitude and my emotions unpredictable?

Did these questions help you discover anything about yourself? Here's the good news—having some boundaries is not only okay, it's necessary. You can say no. You don't have to rescue everyone; instead, you can develop solid, healthy, give-and-take friendships. You can be the woman God created you to be and actually enjoy life instead of constantly overloading yourself with other people's expectations.

But it's not going to happen like magic. You and I must relearn how to do relationships.

> Boundaries are to protect life, not to limit pleasures.
> **EDWIN LOUIS COLE**

Have you ever felt trapped in other people's expectations? *If I say no, she won't be my friend anymore. He'll dump me, for sure. Dad will be mad at me if I don't...*

And so we say yes one more time. Every ill-advised yes is like a stick we're adding to the fire of our own frustration—a fire that rages up seemingly out of nowhere in anger, cutting remarks, and aggressive behavior.

Ever wondered why we girls can be so crazy and unpredictable? It often goes back to a string of yeses. Sure, we may say yes with a smile, but every time we feel as if our rights have been violated, we feed that inner fire. Inside, we're irritated and annoyed. We may feel put upon or used, or we may think life is just that way.

But regardless of what frustrations we girls are feeling, we stuff our concerns deep in our hearts. Guilt drives our actions because when we say no, we feel like horrible, heartless people. So in the name of serving others, we let other people walk all over us. We invite them to take advantage of us, use our stuff, and borrow our money, our car, our notes...

Meeting other people's needs may sound good and godly, but if that's the goal of our lives, we may be missing out on what God wants for us as His girls. How it must hurt King Jesus' heart to watch His bride willingly enslave herself to other people's desires as if we were God.

You and I may think we're serving and loving our friends, but if we help people out just so we don't feel horrible and guilty about ourselves, we're really just using them. Sure, we may not realize it, but the truth is, you and I may be helping people just so we can feel better about ourselves.

Okay, great, Megan, you might be thinking. *But what am I supposed to do? My friends expect me to do stuff for them. All the time. How do I know what the healthy balance is? I mean, I really do care about them. I don't just want to check out.*

And you're right. The key here is balance. Robert Burney, a psychologist who knows a whole lot more about this stuff than I do, put it this way:

> The purpose of having boundaries is to protect and take care of ourselves. We need to be able to tell other people when they are acting in ways that are not acceptable to us. A first step is starting to know that we have the right to protect and defend ourselves. That we have not only the right, but the duty to take responsibility for how we allow others to treat us.[3]

I *love* helping my friends out. But I have learned that if I don't take care of myself, I can't take care of anybody else. As God's girls, we are respon-sible to take care of ourselves.

Of course, I'm not talking a bunch of love-yourself-and-forget-about-everybody-else sassiness. As God's girls, we should care about other people. We should desire to help and serve. But when we throw ourselves into helping other people without taking care of ourselves—without resting, without enjoying life—a breakdown is ahead.

Your Ticket Out

We girls often live without boundaries for several misguided reasons:

- We can believe that neglecting ourselves to help other people is what God wants. So we always say yes to any request because we want to please God.

- We can draw our identity from rescuing other people, from being strong. So we stuff our own problems and pain, and we overwork ourselves. Our time and energy is focused on mak-ing everybody else okay.

- We are afraid that if we say no, our friends won't love us any-more. So we think that saying no is really saying, "I don't love you. Get out of my life."

Are you a bit like Spastic Sam? Actually, every girl has to face the strug-gle of setting healthy boundaries. They don't just pop up like magic!

Maybe saying yes has led you to compromise with a guy, and now you hate yourself for being so naive. Maybe your life is overloaded, chaotic, and out of control because you're trying to do a million and one things, and there's just not enough time in the day. Maybe your addiction to say-ing yes has stolen the joy out of your life. Maybe you overcommitted your-self, and now you're burned out on life—and God. You've gotten to the point where you feel flat and lacking energy.

God had a reason for creating you as a caring person, and the world needs your compassionate heart. But let's build some balance. What do healthy boundaries look like in real life? Rather than putting us in bondage, boundaries free us up to enjoy life and serve better. Rather than constantly striving to meet other people's unrealistic expectations, we can be our-selves. Boundaries let us define who we are and who we aren't. What we'll do and what we won't do. In the moment, when we're faced with a decision, boundaries help us to see more clearly what is right and what is wrong.

Like the barrier that protects us from the lions and the bears and the monkeys at the zoo, or the fence that keeps the kids on the playground safe, boundaries are good and helpful. Without a barrier, the zoo would be a scary and dangerous place. Without a fence, the playground next to the highway would not be a safe place to play.

In the same way, when you and I try to live without boundaries because we think we're strong enough or smart enough to make decisions on the fly, we're just lying to ourselves. Let's be realistic. No girl can do it all, not even Miss America or the First Lady, and definitely not you or me. So what's a girl to do?

Understand Why You Can't Say No

Our first step toward living free as God's girls is to examine our own hearts. Why are you doing the things that you're doing? To make other people happy? To dull the voices of guilt in your own heart? Sometimes parents or friends put conditions on their love or friendship. Our desire for their approval gives them an incredible amount of power in shaping the way we think and act.

Maybe you grew up in a family without boundaries. A lot of my friends have watched their parents divorce, and that's hard. Sometimes we feel as if everything we rely on is pulled out from under our feet, and we fall. Hard. The instability of a broken family can lead a lot of us girls into a pattern of just wanting others to like and love us, so we perform for them. We dance and serve because if we don't, people won't be there for us. They won't love us—or so we think.

Find Your Stability in God

When life hurts, you and I need a safe place. No girl can be strong all the time, and stuffing the pain and hurt inside doesn't help one bit. When life doesn't make sense, when everything around us spins out of control, the only safe place to run is into Jesus' arms.

Over and over and over again, the Bible promises us that God will be there for us, that He'll never leave us. When we girls ponder these promises, we will gradually become convinced that we don't have to freak out, even when we feel out of control.

- "God is a safe place to hide, ready to help when we need him" (Psalm 46:1).

- "Even when the way goes through Death Valley, I'm not afraid when you walk at my side" (Psalm 23:4).

- "GOD is bedrock under my feet, the castle in which I live, my rescuing knight" (Psalm 18:1).

- "Everything I need comes from him...He's solid rock under my feet, breathing room for my soul" (Psalm 62:1-2).

Honestly, sometimes you and I need to just rest. Not work, not strive, not serve—just rest and let Jesus carry us. Regardless of what's going on in our lives, God is always faithful and trustworthy. His love is unconditional. We can pour out our hearts to Him and know that He hears every whisper and every longing.

Take Care of Yourself

God's girl does care about and serve and love other people. But at the same time, she doesn't hate herself. The Bible commands us to love our neighbor (Matthew 19:18), but if we don't respect, value, and love ourselves, we'll go through life willing to do anything just to feel loved.

Take some time to look over your schedule. Do you set aside time to rest? To talk to God? To get in His Word? To take a bubble bath or go out for a jog? If every second of our day is jammed-packed with doing, chances are we need to set some healthy boundaries. People will always need you. There will always be somebody to talk to, somebody to pray with.

But even Jesus (who was God!) set aside a good chunk of time to spend with God. Not doing, working, or serving—just being. The Bible tells us that even when thousands of needy people followed Jesus and His disciples, Jesus took a break.

"Come with me by yourselves to a quiet place and get some rest," Jesus said to His disciples (Mark 6:31 NIV). And you know what? He's saying the same thing to you and me.

We young women can easily get caught up in the rat race of our culture. But God wants so much more for you and me. He wants to reveal to us the deep, intimate, life-changing truths of His Word. Spending time with Jesus is not a duty or an obligation. It's the biggest privilege in the whole wide world.

Could any girl in her right mind say she's too busy for that?

Ask for Advice

Trying to figure life out on our own can be pretty confusing and overwhelming. Sometimes, as we're trying to set boundaries in our lives—and to figure out what to say no to—the input of older, wiser people can be really helpful.

I used to think I could do life solo, but every day I realize more and more that a lot of times, despite our brave fronts, you and I have some blind spots. That's why we desperately need people who've "been there, done that" to help us see life better and establish realistic and healthy boundaries. As the wise man said, "Without good direction, people lose their way; the more wise counsel you follow, the better your chances" (Proverbs 11:14).

Whom do you go to for advice? Sure, we all ask our friends, but sometimes they don't know much more than we do. Maybe it's a youth pastor, a small group leader, a teacher, or our parents. If you and I don't have at least one person we look up to, someone we can go to for advice, it's time to start praying and hunting. God knows exactly what you need. Don't be ashamed to ask around. Talk to your pastor, your parents, or your youth group leader. Seek out people whom you want to become like and value their advice.

In the Word

Why does God's girl set boundaries and respect herself? Because she knows that she is precious and valuable—not because of what she does, but because she is created in the image of God. The apostle Paul wrote, "You are not your own; you were bought at a price. Therefore honor God with your body" (1 Corinthians 6:19-20). As God's girls, you and I aren't our own free agents. We exist for one reason: to bring glory to God. To point people back to Jesus.

Jesus paid for our freedom with His own blood. That makes us pretty precious, doesn't it! So setting boundaries, telling other people no sometimes, isn't just about protecting ourselves from burnout and heartbreak. It's about honoring God.

When we live free as God's girls, we're driven by love, not fear. By genuine humility, not self-abasement. We help and serve others not to ward off feelings of guilt, not to feel good about ourselves, but because God is overflowing in our lives.

Serving other people becomes a privilege because we get to partner with God in His work. But God's girl has a realistic view of herself. She doesn't carry the weight of the world on her shoulders. That's God's deal. She doesn't think that if she says no, the stars will fall out of the sky. "We neither make nor save ourselves. God does both the making and saving. He creates each of us by Christ Jesus to join him in the work he does, the good work he has gotten ready for us to do, work we had better be doing" (Ephesians 2:10).

Every day, God's girl loves and gives and serves. But she doesn't kill herself trying to prove something. She serves out of love.

This world is needy, and you and I can't meet all those needs. We could invest ourselves in a lot of good things, but we can't do it all. As God's girls, we need wisdom to discern the difference between good things and God things. If you and I want to invest our lives in God things, we're going to have to say no to some really good things along the way.

You and I aren't slaves working in God's kitchen. We're God's daughters. We have the joy and privilege of walking with our heavenly Father every day, of joining Him in the work He does. Who wouldn't want that?

> Your personal boundaries protect the
> inner core of your identity.
> **GERARD MANLEY HOPKINS**

Smart Girls Remember...

- If you define yourself by what you do, your life will be crazy and unpredictable.
- You don't exist to fix other people. Only God can do that.
- Be careful what you say yes to, because it will control you.

- You're not a superwoman. You can't do everything. Wisdom helps sort out the good things and the God things.
- Saying no isn't always the selfish thing to do. Sometimes, saying no is godly.

———

God,

My life is out of control. I live in the moment and do whatever I want, but I'm starting to realize that this isn't a good or healthy way to live. I spend most of my time trying to make everybody happy. I try to fix their problems. And God, I just can't do it anymore. I'm tired of being the strong one. I need rest. Give me wisdom to set healthy boundaries instead of letting other people walk all over me. I want to live for You, God. I want to bring You glory. Help me to trust You to work instead of trying to do it all on my own.

Amen.

9

Can't Let Her Hair Down

Just relax. Just trust. You need to learn how to trust.

NOAH IN *THE NOTEBOOK*

T*he Proposal* introduces us to the world of Margaret Tate, a master-of-the-universe publishing executive who runs a tight ship. No grace, no compliments, no smile, and not a moment to relax.

And everyone hates her. The moment Miss Tate's black heels hit the office floor, the conversations stop. No more jokes, no more laughter.

"The witch is on her broom," Andrew Paxton hastily instant messages to the office staff. Simultaneously, they paste on serious faces, hunch over a bit, grab their phones, lower their eyes to avoid her gaze, and begin to type like crazy. Nobody wants to get on Miss Tate's bad side. She's all business. Driven, uptight, bad-tempered, and demanding. Go against this boss, and you'll be standing on the street corner. Just ask Bob Spaulding.

But at least Bob tells the truth: "Just because you have no semblance of a life outside of this office, you think you can treat all of us like your own personal slaves. You know what? I feel sorry for you. Because you know what you're gonna have on your deathbed? Nothing and no one."

"I have work to do," Margaret snaps as she hurries down the hall toward her office.

Whew—talk about intense! Ever had a boss or a friend like that? Driven to the extreme, uptight, and buried in her schoolwork? Always busy, always going, always serving, and always striving to do better? She never cracks a smile. *Holy* and *obedient* are her favorite words. She's completely forgotten how to live.

She doesn't have a clue as to how to enjoy life, relax, tell a good joke, or belly laugh at one. She can't dance, can't let down her hair and just *be*. To a

|41|

woman like Margaret, those things simply waste time. Margaret's life is all about accomplishment, making the grade, and getting to the top.

Sound familiar? Has anyone ever told you that being godly meant being serious? That following God meant embracing a hard life of blood, sweat, and tears and not joyful obedience? That being spiritual is all about being somber, staid, and cautious? That making a B was the same as failing? That goofing off with friends, running through the grass barefoot, and laughing till you can't breathe is immature?

In this chapter, we're going to dive headfirst into these big fat lies. Together, we're going to rediscover who God created us to be as His daughters—full of joy, running free, and delighting in our God.

> Joy is the feeling of grinning inside.
> **MELBA COLGROVE**

Defining *Uptight*

What is an uptight girl like? According to one dictionary, she's "tense, nervous, and strictly conventional; without joy or gladness." Maybe she's worried about messing up. Worried about making God mad. For whatever reason, she's driven by obligation and fear.

On the flip side, we all want to achieve something in life. What girl wants to get to her last breath and say, "Woulda, shoulda, coulda"? Not me! But a joyless girl thinks that having fun is somehow wrong. It's immature. She's convinced that the only thing in life that's worthwhile is work or maybe being in total control.

And so she works, works, and works, convinced that she's better than her friends who occasionally break into random dance. Who sing at the top of their lungs in the car. Or who have a sleepover on Friday night when *she* is going to a Bible study.

We girls can easily confuse being composed with following God, especially in Christian circles. We think that being grown up is the same as being godly. We think that being serious and somber makes God notice us.

So what do we do? We box up our favorite comedies. We squelch our laughter. We forget how to have fun. We bury our smiles deep under lists of dos and don'ts. We view enjoyment as evil, and we embrace a life of drudgery. We equate goodness and holiness with following the rules. We can have a really messed-up idea of living for God!

The tragedy of an uptight, joyless life is that you and I forget that Jesus came to set us free. Jesus wasn't a big fan of the Pharisees…the people who were uptight, put together, and super religious. Growing up in a religious environment, we can easily confuse religion with a real, personal, vibrant, passionate relationship with Jesus.

When we girls are constantly worried about performing and measuring up, we miss out on a lot of the joy of being human. Of being God's girls. We tend to…

> worry about how other people see us
>
> be proud about our own righteousness
>
> forget how to relax and enjoy life's blessings
>
> associate fun with sin
>
> judge other girls as spiritually immature
>
> lack joy in our everyday lives
>
> define our spirituality by all the stuff we don't do
>
> work for God without really knowing Him

Worst of all, we girls often live narrow, boring, abstract lives…and call it Christianity. We load ourselves down with man-made, cultural rules about what's appropriate and what's not instead of really living the way Jesus would. And we give our friends and the world the idea that following God is a burden, a chore, a bunch of nose-to-the-grindstone work.

What a horrible way to live! No wonder so many girls don't want anything to do with following Jesus. We've lived a lie, we've followed empty rules, and we've forgotten God.

> A sense of humor isn't for everyone. It's only for people who want to have fun, enjoy life, and feel alive.
> **ANNE WILSON SCHAEF**

Getting to Know Jammed-Up Janna

"Whadaya doing tonight? A bunch of us girls are going to a game night at Kaylee's house. Wanna come with?" I asked my friend Janna as we headed to class.

"No, but thanks for asking. I'm not really into games and stuff. Besides, I've got to study for my test next week."

"But Janna, you *always* study. Don't you need a break sometime?"

"Oh, I do take breaks. I go to Bible study on Thursday nights."

"That's awesome. But what about…like, ya know…just chill time? You time."

Janna gave me a rather blank stare. "Uh…that's not really my thing, Megan. When I'm not doing school, I'm usually getting ready for teaching Awanas and Sunday school."

"Wait, you teach Awanas *and* Sunday school?"

"Yeah, you know," Janna shrugged her shoulders. "I mean, I want my life to count for something. I wanna leave my mark, Megan."

Wow. Janna was really serious about this. All I wanted to do was invite her to play some board games with us!

"Honestly, hanging out just seems like a waste of time to me," Janna said with the subtlest hint of superiority.

Later the same week, I ran into Janna at lunch sitting by herself. "Hey girl, do you mind if I join you?"

"Sure," Janna smiled, moving her backpack to make room.

"So, what's going on?" I asked her. "How did that test turn out?"

"Oh, it's next week. I was just getting a head start on it."

"Wow, that's great! You know, Janna, I really admire your commitment to school. I mean, some girls barely pass, but you…you take it really seriously. But girl, I've been thinking about what you said the other day, and I'm just wondering. Do you really think that hanging out and just having fun is like, wrong?"

Janna thought about it for a second. "I dunno, Megan. I mean, I want to please God with my life. I guess I just always thought that being a good Christian meant…you know, digging into the Word. Praying. Helping other people. Not doing all the stuff that *they* do.

"My mom always told me growing up that fun leads to compromise," Janna continued. "That God wants us to be serious and sober-minded. To think deep thoughts and not waste our time on stupid stuff."

GIRLS LIKE YOU AND ME HAD THIS TO SAY ABOUT BEING UPTIGHT...

"If we are so stressed out that we can't enjoy the little blessings of life—sunsets, flowers, birds singing—then we're too busy."
—MARY

"We all need chill time. Following God doesn't mean we have to be on our knees every single moment. It *does* mean that whatever we do (that's not sin) can be worship."
—KATELYN

"We have a lot of misconceptions about following God. He didn't come to enslave us to rules. He came to set us free to run after Him."
—CARLEE

"Joy isn't something we magically wake up with. We have to fight for it by changing our perspective of what's really important in life."
—LAKEN

"One of the biggest marks of spiritual maturity is confidence in who we are in Christ. The girl who really knows Jesus is okay with herself. She can relax, chill, goof off even. She knows that it's not up to her to save the world."
—BETH

"Learn to laugh at yourself. It's the best medicine against depression."
—JOSIE

In Janna's mind, having fun was sinful. I ache to see my friend go through life believing this lie. I respect Janna a ton. She knows God's Word, and she's really wise. But when it comes to everyday life, Janna can't relate. She's all work and no play!

Come to think about it, I've rarely seen Janna laugh. Or goof off. When she walks into the room, she usually sucks out all of the fun, and conversations often turn into theological debates. The only dance Janna knows is the good-girl dance, and it looks kind of weird. Janna isn't comfortable with herself at all. She's always worried about looking silly, so she opts out of games, parties, and anything that appears to her to be unspiritual.

Talk about depressing!

Why do so many of us get so messed up in this area? Why is it so hard for some of us to relax and just enjoy life? We try too hard, try to be perfect, try to impress other people with our best "spiritual" face. But living this way can leave us lonely, confused, and desperate for something to change.

If we are constantly worried about what we have to do, how to do it well, or what other people think, we can drive ourselves crazy. Living like this steals our joy and even damages our health. Anxiety is a big issue for women in America. In fact, anxiety issues are twice as common for girls as for guys. That's a lot of worry. A lot of fear. Anxiety is a very real issue for many of us girls. And when we try to stuff it so we can maintain our spiritual, put-together image, we just get *more* anxious.

Stress or anxiety can eat a girl alive from the inside out. In fact, stress is one of the biggest issues that students face. According to a recent poll…

- 85 percent of students say they are stressed on a daily basis.
- 77 percent of teens stress about schoolwork.
- Over half of students say they've been so stressed that they couldn't finish their work.[1]

Sure, we girls may try to be strong. But pretending only goes so far. Stuffing our feelings isn't healthy. At all. Behind our masks, we all find ways to cope. We run, we overeat, we shop until we drop, we zone out on Facebook…but one of the best ways to fight stress and anxiety is to laugh. Here's what Richard Swenson says. He's an expert on stress:

> By the time babies are four months old, they already are laughing once every hour. And by the age of four years, these clowns laugh on average once every four minutes—or four hundred times a day. By the time we reach adulthood, however, we manage only fifteen laughs a day.[2]

How many times a day do you laugh? Are you so uptight that you've lost your sense of humor? Following God doesn't mean being dull and boring. After all, laughter is God's idea. He created pleasure, fun, excitement, and joy.

> Joy in one's heart and some laughter on one's lips is a
> sign that the person has a pretty good grasp of life.
> **HUGH SIDNEY**

Jammed-Up Janna and You

"Fun leads to compromise." Janna's idea of following God seemed to include being miserable. Somewhere along the way, she got the messed-up idea that pleasure was evil, that being a good Christian meant always being composed.

What about you? Does Janna's story sound familiar? Are you taking life too seriously? Is a sense of duty draining the joy out of your life? Maybe these open-ended questions can help you find out.

Am I often stressed out? Am I a worrywart?

Do I tend to take on more than I can handle?

Is my life driven by joy or by obligation?

Am I serious all the time?

Can I turn off the stress and just relax?

When was the last time I laughed at myself?

When was the last time I played?

Do I feel guilty whenever I have fun?

Do I worry a lot about my image?

Am I always short on time?

Did you find any signs of too much stress in your life? Here's the good news: You don't have to be stressed and anxious all the time. You can experience real, true joy. You can relax and enjoy the little blessings of life. You don't have to fit into a super-serious spiritual mold. God created you and me for so much more than a life of legalism and boredom.

Have you ever looked at your life and gotten a little scared, wondering if you're missing out on something? Do you ever think, *Is this all life is about—work, eat, sleep, and repeat?* Does your life seem to be filled with more rules than joy? A lot of us don't even realize this is the way we're living.

God wants so much more for us as His daughters. I love this quote by C.S. Lewis:

> We are half-hearted creatures, fooling around with drink and sex and ambition when infinite joy is offered us, like an ignorant child who wants to go on making mud pies in a slum because he cannot imagine what is meant by the offer of a holiday at the sea. We are far too easily satisfied. [3]

Are you spending your life making mud pies with all the seriousness and concentration a kid can muster? Left to ourselves, we will live small, empty, meaningless lives. We often pour our time and energy into stuff that doesn't really matter. We run after anything that feels good, even if it destroys us. We choose the mud of empty religion instead of the entire ocean of who God is!

Sound depressing? It is. Without God intervening, we would miss a lot of the life and freedom He has for us. Even our best attempts at being good, at trying to please God, are like mud pies compared to the power and grandeur of the ocean of God's power and holiness. Let's quit striving and start enjoying our freedom in Christ!

Empty religion and man-made rules just won't cut it. We may put every single ounce of our strength into being good or holy, doing what's right and staying away from sin. But at the end of it all, when we stand before God, our efforts will not be enough.

God is perfect, so His very character requires us to be perfect 100 percent of the time, 24/7.

But here's our cause for joy. You and I have been rescued from this hopeless, tragic end by the blood of Jesus. Here's the deal:

It wasn't so long ago that you were mired in that old stagnant life of sin. You let the world, which doesn't know the first thing about living, tell you how to live. You filled your lungs with polluted unbelief, and then exhaled disobedience. We all did it, all of us doing what we felt like doing, when we felt like doing it, all of us in the same boat. It's a wonder God didn't lose his temper and do away with the whole lot of us. Instead, immense in mercy and with an incredible love, he embraced us. He took our sin-dead lives and made us alive in Christ (Ephesians 2:1-5).

When you and I choose to follow Jesus Christ, everything radically changes. No, I'm not talking about fireworks in the sky and warm fuzzies inside. I'm talking about reality. The apostle Peter puts it this way: "You were redeemed from the empty way of life handed down to you...with the precious blood of Christ, a lamb without blemish or defect" (1 Peter 1:18-19 NIV).

Regardless of the stresses or pressures that come at God's girl, she doesn't have to freak out. Never. God's girl has been rescued, and her sins have been forgiven. She has a purpose in life, and it's not to be solemn, serious, and put-together. No way. Our purpose is to delight in God. To revel in Him. To find our joy and pleasure in Him. King David knew what this is about.

> You have made known to me the path of life;
>> you will fill me with joy in your presence,
>> with eternal pleasures at your right hand (Psalm 16:11 NIV).

Joy is not something you and I can muster up on our own, regardless of how hard we try. Our joy comes from God Himself, and it's not just a feeling.

God is offering us not just "a holiday at the sea," but eternity in His presence. Perfect love. Perfect joy. Perfect delight. It's way better than anything our minds can even imagine.

And it starts now.

If you've been living life uptight, thinking that following God means being completely serious, solemn, and grim...well, it's time to think again. As God's girls, we have every reason to be the happiest and freest people in the whole wide world. Romans 6:14,18 (NIV) says, "You are not under law, but under grace…You have been set free from sin."

We are redeemed from the bondage of sin! God has given you and me the privilege of knowing Him intimately. *He* is our joy.

For just a moment, forget about making the grade, striving to do better, accomplishing everything you can, and being put-together and mature and grown up and holy. Let's lose this misconceived view of spirituality once and for all!

> I sometimes wonder whether all pleasures are substitutes for joy.
> **C.S. LEWIS**

Your Ticket Out

As girls, we can be uptight and overly serious for several reasons.

- We can confuse composure and a false view of maturity with really knowing Jesus. So we squelch our emotions and hide behind a perfectly put-together facade.

- We can find our identity in legalistic rules and judge every other girl as worldly if she doesn't fit with our idea of spirituality.

- We think that having fun, hanging out, and belly laughing are shallow and worthless, so we throw ourselves into work without a moment's rest.

What's a girl to do? Maybe as you've been reading, you've realized that you're a little like Jammed-Up Janna. Especially in Christian circles, you and I have got to battle the lie that being serious and being spiritual are one and the same. To live in God's joy, we need to start each day not by thinking about everything we have to do, but by stepping back and taking a look at what God has already done for us. Just about anytime we get overwhelmed, anxious, or stressed out, we've probably taken our eyes off of Jesus.

What does a girl look like who is filled with God's joy? Instead of being uptight, jammed up, and stressed out, we can be calm, peaceful, and content. Full of life, free, and fun. A girl who lives this way knows that following God is about loving Him and obeying Him, not conforming to some man-made set of dos and don'ts. She delights in God. She's busy loving life rather than merely existing.

And she feels the freedom to express herself, whether that means breaking out into random song or breaking the silence with uproarious laughter. The joy of the Lord is her strength. Her life is an example. It's a testimony to how good and faithful and amazing the God she follows really is. Joy, not duty, defines this girl's life. And she draws other people like a magnet because they want the same freedom.

How can we girls actually live like that—free, confident, and delighting in Jesus?

Refine Your Idea of Following Jesus

Our culture can give us a pretty messed-up understanding of how to really follow God. Being a Christian is more than going to church, following rules, or missing out on all the fun in life. I love this quote by Josh McDowell: "Going to church doesn't make you a Christian any more than walking into McDonald's makes you a Big Mac."

How ridiculous would it be to think that you and I were Happy Meals just because we walked into a McDonald's lobby! Amazingly, though, this is how we often think about our relationship with God. It's easy for us to think that being serious and uptight pleases God, because so many people who call themselves Christians act that way.

But as we've seen in this chapter, it's not true! A relationship with God is personal and real, not abstract and otherworldly. It's a vibrant, passionate, joy-filled, day-to-day reality.

Following Jesus means choosing to run after God's desires, not our own. "Let us throw off everything that hinders and the sin that so easily entangles, and let us run with perseverance the race marked out for us. Let us fix our eyes on Jesus" (Hebrews 12:1-2 NIV).

You in?

Learn to Delight in God

As God's girls, we should delight in one thing—Jesus. King David agreed: "Delight yourself in the LORD and he will give you the desires of your heart" (Psalm 37:4 NIV). Of course, God is not a genie in a bottle, so this verse is not saying that if we delight in Jesus, we'll get everything we want. Not at all. In fact, if you and I got everything we wanted, we'd probably be some pretty messed-up people!

So what's the point? God's girls realize that the only thing—or rather, the only person—big enough to truly satisfy our hearts is Jesus Christ Himself. Not success, not popularity, and not guys. Delighting in God means that we find our joy, our fulfillment, and our significance in Him. It's way bigger than just following rules or trying to be good!

The girl who delights in God isn't crazy to get guys' attention. She doesn't freak out if she gets a C on a test rather than an A. She doesn't define herself by her hair, her makeup, or her clothes (though God did make us to be beautiful!). She doesn't allow the monster of comparison to make her feel less-than or no good.

The word *delight* describes more than just a feeling. Every day, God's girl reminds herself of the privilege she has to know Jesus intimately. It's so easy for me to take that for granted and forget that before the cross, you and I—and every other girl who has ever lived—were dead in our sins and enemies of God.

Delighting in God means making Him the center of our everyday life. Whatever we're doing—school, work, hanging out with friends, chores, going on a date, watching a movie, surfing the Internet—we can delight in God by taking joy in the gifts He gives to us and by talking to Him about whatever's going on.

Loosen Up a Bit

The freedom Jesus offers us is a far cry from the stuffy, serious persona and the religiosity we have talked about in this chapter. When you and I begin to grasp the reality of our blessings in Jesus Christ, we can't possibly mope our way through life and keep a straight face. And there's no room for a pasted-on smile either. Joy comes from the realization of who we are, whose we are, and what we've been rescued from. *That* is sure to put a skip in your step and a song in your heart.

David "danced with great abandon before GOD" (2 Samuel 6:14). Life before our amazing God should be exuberant, undignified, and passionate. Let's stop holding back and start giving Him all we've got!

Live the Life God Created You to Live

God's not a fan of our modern conception of piety. He's after our passion, our hearts. So rather than conforming to a rule book and finding our identity in good works, we can express our love for God through our everyday, walking-around lives.

The Bible puts it this way: "A man can do nothing better than to eat and drink and find satisfaction in his work. This too, I see, is from the hand of God, for without him, who can eat or find enjoyment?" (Ecclesiastes 2:24-25 NIV).

We Christians are always tempted to take pride in our own righteousness, but that will lead us to live lonely, isolated, safe lives guided by empty rules. Maybe it's time we learned to glorify God—to worship Him—not only through our work but also through our play!

So stop. Take a break. Don't take yourself or your life too seriously. Ditch your chemistry book for the night. Grab a few good friends and go find some good, clean fun.

Your laughter and play make God smile. After all, He is the source of your joy.

In the Word

Look at Habakkuk 3:17:

> Though the cherry trees don't blossom
> and the strawberries don't ripen,
> Though the apples are worm-eaten
> and the wheat fields stunted,
> Though the sheep pens are sheepless
> and the cattle barns empty...

Stop right there for a moment. You and I may not have cherry trees, strawberries, wheat fields, or cattle barns, but we do have certain expectations in life. Just as the children of Israel expected the wheat to grow and the fruit to ripen, you and I expect to have loving parents, trustworthy friends, and a godly boyfriend. We expect good grades that will lead to a dream job and a nice house. And on and on it goes.

But the point of this verse is that our joy doesn't depend on stuff. It doesn't depend on having fancy clothes, being in a relationship, or even making good grades. As Christians, our joy is rooted in the joy of God, not in what God does for us.

That's where we girls go wrong sometimes. We feel excited or happy and confuse our emotions with true joy. But true joy goes far deeper than our present circumstances. And by the way, God doesn't owe us anything— nothing at all! So when you and I get mad and frustrated because we're not getting what we want, we're acting like spoiled little kids. When we ignore God and go off to our corner and pout, we're forgetting the whole deal about joy. What's the deal?

You and I deserve eternal judgment and separation from God. Forever. But God offers us life in His presence. Forever. Um…who's complaining? So let's pick up where we left off:

> I'm singing joyful praise to GOD.
> I'm turning cartwheels of joy to my Savior God.
> Counting on GOD's Rule to prevail,
> I take heart and gain strength (verses 18-19).

When was the last time you burst into song because you were so happy, so overwhelmed with how amazing God was?

Did you get your "cartwheels of joy" in for the day yet?

Do you gain your strength for each day from your own reserves, or from God?

Let's get at it! Let's kick the stuffy, serious life to the gutter and actually start living as if we were forgiven, as if we were redeemed, as if we were free.

Because we are!

Joy is the holy fire that keeps our purpose
warm and our intelligence aglow.
HELEN KELLER

Smart Girls Remember...

- Laughter is one of the best ways to release stress and anxiety.
- God did not create you to live a stuffy, serious, somber life. He's the source of all joy.
- Following God will free you up to live in joy rather than duty.
- The most important thing to focus on is delighting in God.
- Jesus doesn't want you to merely talk about joy, think about joy, or read about joy. He longs for you to dive deep into His joy and find your strength there.

Hey God,

I think I'm finally getting it—what Your life is all about. It's not about trying, not about proving, not about gaining Your approval. Teach me how to delight in You, God. I'm tired of playing games and riding on my emotions. I want to live in Your joy every single day instead of relying on my own strength. God, show me the balance between having fun and being serious. I don't want to live to please other people anymore, God. You are my one audience, and I want to worship You with abandon.

Amen.

10

Living As If God Didn't Matter

*She was a good Christian woman with a large respect for
religion, though she did not, of course, believe any of it was true.*

FLANNERY O'CONNOR

In the early 1800s, a young Englishman traveled to California in search of gold. After several months of prospecting, he struck it rich. On his way home he stopped in New Orleans. Not long into his visit, he came upon a crowd of people and realized that they had gathered for a slave auction.

A young girl was pushed up on the platform and poked and prodded so everyone could get a good look at her. Her nearly naked body was covered with sweat, glistening under the summer sun. The miner could tell she was once beautiful, but she had obviously been beaten. Her wounds oozed, and infection was setting in.

The bidding began.

Soon the bids surpassed what all but two of the slaveholders would pay. The bidding continued higher and higher as these two fought over her as if she were a piece of meat. Finally, one man bid a price that was beyond the reach of the other. The slave girl's eyes were downcast. In just a few minutes, she'd once again be abused as the property of a cruel man.

"Going once, going twice..." The auctioneer called out.

No longer able to control his righteous anger, the English miner sprang to his feet and doubled the previous bid. The onlookers laughed, thinking the miner was only joking. But they grew silent as he strode through the crowd with a bag of gold.

The slave girl shuffled off the platform, her chains clinking with every step, to meet her newest owner. She could only expect more of the same brutality she had experienced with each of her previous masters. Eye to eye with the miner, seething with rage, she spit in his face. Without a word,

157

the miner wiped his face, paid the auctioneer, took the girl by the hand, and led her away from the stunned crowd, where he removed her chains.

They continued walking in silence until they came to a government building. The miner led the slave girl inside, where she sat and waited while he met with an employee. Minutes later, he returned and handed her some papers. "Here," he said simply. "You're now a free woman."

Stunned and confused, the girl looked at the papers, not yet willing to believe that he was telling the truth. "You just bought me, and now you're setting me free?"

"That's why I bought you," he replied. "To set you free."

If you were this girl, how would you respond? What would you do? Would you ignore the man who bought you? Go through your life as if he never existed?

Never before had the slave girl felt the thrill of freedom. Who was this man? He paid a huge price to provide her with a new life, and in his presence she was safe. She had only one response: "I will follow you the rest of my life."

But a lot of us girls live our lives as if God were not really there. We may call ourselves Christians, but our lives are all about us. We live as if God were just a nice Sunday school character.

As you've been reading the pages of this book, what's been going on in your own heart? I wish we could sit down over a cup of Starbucks and talk it all out, but all we have is these few pages.

Girls like You and Me

All of us girls are on the same journey toward womanhood, toward life, toward God. We are dealing with the same struggles. We're trying to avoid the same mistakes. Sure, maybe we live thousands of miles away from each other, but our hearts yearn for the same things. We want to be loved, to be cherished. We want to know that we're beautiful and worth fighting for. We want stability and a safe place to rest when our emotions go haywire. We want to dream God-sized dreams and make a difference in our world.

We want to feel significant—to live for more than our own petty little lives. We want to be accepted, to be approved. We want to make somebody proud. We want to be confident and to know who we are. We want to belong, to enjoy rich friendships, to be special to somebody. We want to experience true intimacy, to be known and loved despite our flaws. We want someone to desire us, to delight in us, to rejoice over us.

And just like the slave girl, we want to be free. Free to be real. Free to be ourselves instead of hiding. Free to take off our masks, break away from other people's opinions, and really live life.

What girl doesn't want all that?

As I've prayed and cried and written this little book, my desire has been simply that you would know Jesus in an increasingly personal and intimate relationship that will last forever. I'm not talking about just praying a prayer or walking the aisle.

Do you believe in God, dear friend? Ninety percent of Americans do. But believing that God exists is a far cry from truly trusting Jesus with all of your life.

Did you grow up in a religious family? Do you go to church? These can be helpful, but they're means to an end. Giving God your life and surrendering to Him is a choice you must make for yourself.

You see, every single one of us girls is born messed up inside. And regardless of how hard we try, we're stuck in our selfishness, our sin, our unholy desires. We're slaves.

The Bible says that "all our righteous acts are like filthy rags" (Isaiah 64:6 NIV). We can never be good enough to live with a perfect God, so we deserve to separated from Him forever.

When you and I come to God, we bring Him *nothing* except our sin, our weaknesses, and our mistakes. That's all we have to offer. Not the best stuff to bargain with, is it?

Fortunately for the slave girl and for us, our futures are not determined by our bargaining power. On the cross, Jesus paid a price far more than all the gold in the world. His death took the punishment for our sins. Every single one.

With Jesus' last words, He made it very clear. "It is finished."

Done. Complete. Finished. You and I can add nothing to His perfect life. So following God isn't a guilt trip or a bunch of rules. No, God is beckoning us, drawing us to Himself. However ugly or no-good you may feel, God wants to rescue you from an empty way of life.

So here's the deal: "If you confess with your mouth, 'Jesus is Lord,' and believe in your heart that God raised him from the dead, you will be saved" (Romans 10:9-10 NIV).

That's it. Following Jesus Christ is a way of life, but it starts with surrendering your heart—and all of who you are—to God. It starts with bringing your sin to Jesus and leaving it there. It starts with repenting, with turning away from a life all about me, my way, and getting what I want.

God is the only one who really satisfies. Sure, drinking, drugs, sex, and being popular may feel good for a while. But only Jesus Christ can satisfy the deepest longings of your soul.

So what about God? How does He fit in?

As your Creator, God hand-fashioned you as His daughter.

As your Sustainer, He continues to give you every breath.

As your Pursuer, God is crazy about you and will never stop loving you.

As your Savior, God—in Jesus—took the punishment for all your sins.

As your Redeemer, God longs to rescue you from the bondage of sin.

As your Shepherd, God promises to guide, protect, and feed you.

As your Father, God is a safe haven you can run to.

As your Friend, God is expectantly waiting to listen to you.

As your Lover, God is head over heels in love with you.

Girl, what are we waiting for! Why are we moping around trying to save ourselves?

What Do You Believe?

Are you God's daughter?

Or have you just been playing games with God? Are you trying to balance out the scales of your good and bad deeds? If you are, you're missing the point. You may be getting by in life—everybody around you may think you're a wonderful person—but when you stand before God one day, what are you going to stand on? Your own righteousness? Not a chance.

Right here, right now, God is calling your name. He's pursuing you, running after your heart. He longs to set you free and give you a brand-new life. Will you let Him?

When you have Christ, all the mistakes we've talked about are covered with His grace. Again and again and again and again. Your life doesn't have to be a crazy race to try to be good enough. Jesus offers you His own righteousness as your own.

God's girl has nothing to lose and nothing to prove. After all, she's adored by Jesus Christ—the King of the entire universe. That's pretty big. Life-shatteringly big.

Following Jesus doesn't mean your life will be easy. No magic pill will stop the pain you and I feel living in a fallen world. But regardless of what happens, a girl who follows Jesus can be confident because she's free. One hundred percent totally and completely free. And she knows that God is always with her.

Francis Chan puts it this way: "God doesn't call us to be comfortable. He calls us to trust Him so completely that we are unafraid to put ourselves in situations where we will be in trouble if He doesn't come through."[1] Because Jesus will always come through for His daughters.

When you and I choose to follow God, He not only forgives us but also starts working on our hearts. He begins changing our desires and transforming the way we think, act, and talk. In love, Jesus begins to chip off all the rough edges and shape us into the women He created us to be.

Sometimes we get frustrated along the way, especially when we blow it. But messing up doesn't mean that you're not a Christian. The closer you and I get to God—the more we know Him—the more we'll see how unworthy we are and how blessed we are to be loved by Him.

There's no question about the end, though. This is what God says: "I'll give you a new heart. I'll put a new spirit in you. I'll cut out your stone heart and replace it with a red-blooded, firm-muscled heart. Then you'll obey my statutes and be careful to obey my commands. You'll be my people! I'll be your God!" (Ezekiel 11:19-20).

Your Ticket Out

So how about it? Are you ready to live as God's girl? A lot of us live with our eyes half open. We stumble along in chains. We try and try and try. But you don't have to.

Maybe you prayed a prayer when you were a kid, and you've just been going through motions. Or maybe you've never surrendered your heart to God. Either way, it doesn't matter. Talk to God right here, right now. Pour out your heart to Him. Tell Him everything that's on your mind. He loves you exactly as you are. He proved your worth with His blood. Jesus paid a tremendous price on the cross to set you free.

And He wants you to live free, to run after Him with all you are, and to delight in being His daughter. So don't hold back. Talk to God, and then go to my Facebook page and send me a note. I can't wait to hear what God is doing in your heart and life. Live free! I'm praying for you.

> I have one desire now—to live a life of reckless abandon for the Lord, putting all my energy and strength into it.
> **ELIZABETH ELLIOT**

Lord Jesus,

I need you. Desperately. On my own, I have nothing. I'm tired of trying to go through life alone, God. I've tried and tried and tried to be good, and I always come up short. I have nothing to bring You except my broken, messed-up life. I want to live for Your glory, not my own deal anymore. I know that I've hurt You a million times with my sin, and I'm so sorry. Will You forgive me? Jesus, will You turn my life into something beautiful? Will You heal me? Please set me free. You're my only hope. I want You to run my life. I'm doing more than praying a prayer, God; I'm giving everything to You. I want to live as Your girl, God. In Jesus' name I pray.

Amen.

Notes

Chapter 1: Crazy for Love

1. Dr. Dean Edell, "Teens Think Oral Sex Is like Abstinence," *Healthcentral.com*, November 16, 2000. www.healthcentral.com/drdean/408/44577.html.

2. Claudia Wallis, "Behavior: A Snapshot of Teen Sex," *Time Magazine*, January 30, 2005. www.time.com/time/magazine/article/0,9171,1022618-1,00.html.

3. Statistics from Students Against Destructive Decisions and from The Heritage Foundation, cited at www.troubledteens.com/troubled-teens-statistics.html.

4. Augustine, *The Confessions of Saint Augustine* (New York: Image Books, 1960), 43.

Chapter 2: Controlled by Emotions

1. Brennan Manning, *Abba's Child* (Colorado Springs: NavPress, 2002), 88-89.

2. Nancy Leigh DeMoss, *Lies Women Believe* (Chicago: Moody, 2002), 200.

Chapter 3: Consumed with Self

1. Julie Scelfo, "Bad Girls Go Wild," *Newsweek*, June 13, 2005. www.newsweek.com/id/50082/page/1.

2. Frank Farley, "Media and Girls," *Media Awareness Network.* www.media-awareness.ca/english/issues/stereotyping/women_and_girls/women_girls.cfm.

Chapter 4: Addicted to Approval

1. Statistics from YWCA, "Beauty at Any Cost." www.ywca.org/site/pp.asp?c=djISI6PIKpG&b=4427615.

2. Cited by the Alliance for Eating Disorders Awareness at www.eatingdisorderinfo.org/Resources/EatingDisordersStatistics/tabid/964/Default.aspx.

3. Ibid.

4. Statistics from Livestrong.com, www.livestrong.com/article/13945-suicide/.

5. Marilyn Elias, "Psychologists now know what makes people happy," *USA Today*, December 8, 2002. www.usatoday.com/news/health/2002-12-08-happy-main_x.htm.

Chapter 5: Chained to Insecurity

1. A.A. Milne, *Winnie the Pooh* (New York: Puffin, 1992), 72.

2. Colette Dowling, "Girls' Dieting and Depression: An Adolescent Crisis," *Women's Wellbeing and Mental Health.* www.womens-wellbeing-and-mental-health.com/girlsdieting.html.

Chapter 7: Drifting Through Life

1. Debra Viadero, "Majority of Youths Found to Lack a Direction in Life," *Education Week*, June 9, 2008. talkgroups-mentors.org/pdfs/statistics/youthfoundtolackdirection%2008.pdf.

2. Ibid.

3. John Piper, *Don't Waste Your Life* (Wheaton: Crossway, 2003), 28.

4. Dominque McKay, "Missionary Heather Mercer tells story of captivity in Afghanistan," Liberty University. www.liberty.edu/index.cfm?PID=18495&MID=5002.

Chapter 8: Living Without Boundaries

1. John Cloud and Henry Townsend, *Boundaries* (Grand Rapids: Zondervan, 1992), 13-14.

2. Evelyn Tehiss, "People who can't say no risk stress, anger and even illness," *Seattle Times*, February 22, 2006. seattletimes.nwsource.com/html/health/2002820091_healthpleasedisease22.html.

3. Robert Burney, *Codependence: The Dance of Wounded Souls* (New York: Joy to Me and You Enterprises, 1995), 5.

Chapter 9: Can't Let Her Hair Down

1. "mtvU AP 2209 Economy, College Stress and Mental Health Poll" www.halfofus.com/_media/_pr/may09_exec.pdf.

2. Richard Swenson, *Margin* (Colorado Springs: NavPress, 2004), 90.

3. C.S. Lewis, *The Weight of Glory* (New York: HarperOne, 2001), 16.

Chapter 10: Living As If God Didn't Matter

1. Francis Chan, *Crazy Love* (Colorado Springs: David C. Cook, 2008), 122.

Other Great Harvest House Books
from Megan Clinton...

Totally God's

Megan and her father, Tim Clinton (president of the American Association of Christian Counselors), shares how your deepest longings are met when you focus on being God's girl. Through comments of peers, Megan's own diary entries, and biblical teachings, you will discover the beauty and freedom of the life of faith.

Totally God's 4 Life Devotional

In this devotional packed with journal entries, everyday stories, and solid biblical application, Megan speaks as one friend to another. In 90 short devotions, she shares from her heart on topics every girl deals with: beauty and body image, crazy emotions, guys and relationships and learning to be totally God's.

...and from Julie Clinton, president of Extraordinary Women

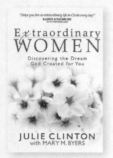

Extraordinary Women

Julie shares biblical illustrations, life examples, and prayers throughout this book. You'll learn to embrace extraordinary living as you discover God's dream for you, make every day count in surprising ways, and release control to take hold of God's freedom.

Living God's Dream for You

Julie shares devotions rich with wisdom gained through her ministry, life, marriage, and faith. Her message will inspire you to grab hold of God's dream for you as you discover the depth of Jesus' love, the wonder of your worth, and the joy of walking in His purpose.

10 Things You Aren't Telling Him

With encouraging examples from her marriage and from women who responded to her survey, Julie models intimacy solutions to help you have important conversations with your husband about your hurts, past secrets, sexual needs, dreams and goals, spiritual needs, and hopes for your marriage.

To learn more about other Harvest House books
or to read sample chapters, log on to our website:

www.harvesthousepublishers.com

HARVEST HOUSE PUBLISHERS

EUGENE, OREGON